A Funny Thing Happened
on the Way to the Boardroom

A Funny Thing Happened on the Way to the Boardroom

Using Humor in Business Speaking

➤ ➤ ➤

Michael Iapoce

WILEY

John Wiley & Sons, Inc.

New York · Chichester · Brisbane · Toronto · Singapore

Publisher: Stephen Kippur
Editor: Katherine Schowalter
Managing Editor: Ruth Greif
Assistant Managing Editor: Corinne McCormick
Editing, Design, Production: Publication Services, Inc.

Library of Congress Cataloging-in-Publication Data

Iapoce, Michael.
  A funny thing happened on the way to the boardroom.
  Using humor in business speaking.

  1. Public speaking.   2. Wit and humor.   I. Title.
PN4193.B8I27   1988   808.5'1'0207   88-10612
ISBN 0-471-63650-9
ISBN 0-471-63649-5 (pbk.)

Printed in the United States of America

88 89 10 9 8 7 6 5 4 3 2 1

To John Cantu,
the unsung guru of comedy

Acknowledgments

There are many people who directly or indirectly contributed to the creation of this book. First and foremost is my agent, Michael Larsen. I thank him for his constant faith, encouragement, and in fact, the actual idea for this project. I must also thank those funny friends who have influenced me from our early days in stand-up comedy to the present—Tom Finnigan, Paul Giles, and John Cantu. Also, my former partners in the world of corporate comedy, Karen Watern and Malcolm Kushner. Last but not least, I thank my wife Ellie for her patience and solid support throughout this (and every other) project.

Preface

This book is not intended to make you a comedian. It *is* intended for both novice and experienced business speakers who have said (or more likely thought), "I'd love to be a little more entertaining when I speak, but I really don't know how." It is for those who have envied the apparently "natural" wit of other speakers but won't try humor in their own presentations because they're afraid they might fail, as in "I'm just not a comedian."

Those are the reservations I've heard most often from executives at all levels in my work as a corporate "humor consultant." It always amazes me. Are there some little-known laws against unauthorized corporate giggling? Has anyone on Wall Street ever been indicted for trading inside jokes? So many otherwise powerful, confident speakers are often hesitant to slip in a light touch—even though they know that it could enhance their image and perhaps even turn an otherwise ordinary speech into a more memorable presentation (i.e., it might help keep the audience awake long enough to hear the speaker's real message). This book is for those people.

Unlike many other humor books, this one is designed to provide basic, how-to instruction in the use of humor, specifically in business or otherwise "serious" settings. If offers numerous helpful hints and examples drawn from both professional comics and successful business speakers that illustrate every aspect of using humor effectively. It also shows how to actually use joke books and other standard sources to suit your purposes. Many speakers complain that the typical joke book contains material that is 99 percent inappropriate, unfunny, or otherwise useless. This book will teach you how to tailor that seemingly unsuitable material into effective humor. It also provides an ample supply of ready-to-use jokes under topical headings that cover the most common areas of business presentations. To paraphrase (a comic's euphemism for "stealing") the automaker's slogan, who could ask for anything more?

I've included extensive instruction on how to deal with any audience—from the preparation of appropriate material to podium delivery techniques. I take special care to detail exactly how to deliver a joke, and to show how the key to being funny lies simply in using your natural sense of humor to be yourself. And if you're not sure of who you are (or who you want to be) at the podium, I'll explain how you can find out by discovering your own "comic persona."

For the speaker or speechwriter who wants to develop proficiency at creating original humor for specific presentations, I reveal many of the surprisingly simple techniques used by professional comedy writers. I explain how to make old jokes new, inappropriate jokes relevant, and dull jokes funny. (Trust me—it's not nearly as difficult as it sounds.) I also offer six basic joke formulas used by professionals to produce a greater volume of material when time is limited.

The second part of the book was written specifically in response to complaints I've heard about the quality of current joke books. You'll notice that I've provided many fewer jokes than typical humor books. Why? Because I firmly believe in sacrificing quantity for quality. After all, no one is really going to use *10,000* jokes, toasts, and stories (and live to tell about it, anyway). I've taken great pains to select from my personal files the funniest jokes on the most relevant topics. All have proven effective in the past with the most resistant audiences. So, I'll go out on a limb and say flat out: These jokes are funny—as long as they're used in the appropriate context.

Some people say that "funny" is a relative, subjective term. This is to some degree true. You personally may not find each and every one of these jokes funny. (*Note:* Please do not call me and ask for explanations. Ask a trusted old friend instead.) Some of them may simply not appear as funny when read out of context as they would when presented in a speech. So in this sense, "funny" can be a relative term. But I prefer the explanation of a comedy associate of mine, John Cantu: "A funny joke is one that gets a laugh. Period." Most of these jokes have been tested under difficult conditions, and only those that have indeed gotten laughs have been included.

Corporate and government speakers, entrepreneurs, fund raisers, seminar leaders, and anyone who must communicate to an audience—as well as speechwriters for all of the above—will find this book a valuable source of practical guidance on how to improve presentations with humor.

The recurring theme of the book, and its single most important bit of information, is simply this: *You don't have to be a natural comedian to use humor effectively.* In fact, humor in business works better if you're not.

So relax.

Contents

3   Delivering Humor with Style   55

7   Stories to Make a Point   168

PART 1

The Skills

The Skills

CHAPTER 1

Laughter Is Cost-Effective

The Value of Humor in Business

This chapter explains the value of humor in business. It uses numerous examples to show how humor:

➢ Connects you to your audience
➢ Eases your approach to sensitive subjects
➢ Disarms a hostile audience
➢ Makes your message easier to understand and remember
➢ Makes your audience more willing to listen

The chapter also confronts and eases the most commonly stated fears about using humor.

When Chrysler was suffering through its darkest days, teetering on the edge of bankruptcy, CEO Lee Iacocca announced that as part of an overall cost-cutting program, he would reduce his own annual salary to one dollar per year. When one of the stockholders questioned the wisdom of this move, Iacocca replied, "Don't worry . . . I spend it very carefully."

In 1984, Ronald Reagan outshone Walter Mondale in one of their debates largely on the basis of his comment on the question of his advanced age: "I promise not to make my opponent's youth and inexperience an issue in this campaign." Even Mondale could only laugh in reply.

While Iacocca and Reagan may hold widely divergent views on a number of issues, these men—two of the most admired leaders in recent American history—obviously agree on one important point: Humor is a valuable tool for influencing people. But even if you're not a chief executive, humor can help distinguish you as more creative, more human, and simply more appealing than the average speaker—in a number of ways.

Humor Makes You One of the Guys—or Gals

Why do you think they call it "sharing" a joke? Humor puts you on common ground with your audience. Since laughter is a most distinctively human behavior, the use of humor lets each audience member know that, whatever the differences in your relative power or status, you are really just like any one of them—a human being.

As a result, they will be more receptive to your message, because people will always tend to be less critical of a fellow human being than they are of a *vice president*, or an *outside consultant*, or even *the speaker*. Let's face it, most introductions of speakers are pretty meaningless to the audience, particularly if they know nothing about you to begin with. And when an unknown quantity's introduction is overly flattering it can have a negative effect, making the audience skeptical and putting them on guard. A humorous opening remark in this situation can reassure listeners and function as a kind of verbal handshake that shows you want to be friends and introduces you as just a regular guy or gal—like each of them. And any time you use humor early on in a speech, you tell the audience that this is going to be different— and better—than the usual presentation, because they can expect some enjoyment from it!

It worked for me when I spoke to a group of marketing consultants who had never heard of me. They were forced to endure a gushing, in-depth recounting of my career by the person who introduced me, and I could almost feel the cool breeze from them as I stepped up to the podium. "Well," I said, "after that introduction, I can hardly wait to hear what I'm going to say."

We all felt better immediately. By humorously expressing our shared feeling, I was able to create a quick bond with the audience—and melt their initial resistance. Humor helps to make the audience want to like the speaker and even want to agree with him—or at least not reject him out of hand. It makes an audience more willing to listen. It's a fact that a spoonful of jokes helps the medicine go down—especially if you're administering a bitter pill.

A Spoonful of Humor Helps the Medicine Go Down

Sometimes it's difficult to get your foot in the door of a sensitive subject without stepping on someone's toes. But the more serious the subject or situation, the more valuable humor can be in easing tensions. Even the most challenging statement sounds less threatening if it's accompanied by a little levity. Remember those old Westerns where cowboys are always saying "Smile when you say that, pardner"? People will more easily accept the tough things that have to be said if there's some humor involved.

One of the most difficult writing assignments I ever had was to create humorous material for the San Francisco Police Department's "Project Safe." Talk about a touchy subject! Police officers would speak to neighborhood groups about what precautions citizens could take to avoid becoming crime victims. Since many of their listeners had already been victimized, they naturally became very serious and tense while hearing about the clever and sometimes unstoppable techniques used by burglars, muggers, and other bad guys. Things would get worse in the question-and-answer session afterward, when people would demand to know why the police weren't doing more to protect them.

It took several rewrites before the captain in charge of the project and I both felt that the jokes were funny enough without being too flippant about a very serious subject. But the extra effort was worth it. Sometimes when things are going to be tense, it's best to simply state the truth of the situation—humorously, of course. When he told an audience things like, "The safest times to walk in Golden Gate Park are 8 A.M., 4 P.M., and midnight . . . that's when the muggers change shifts," or "There's no guaranteed protection against burglary unless you put a deadbolt lock on your door, put a peephole in the door . . . and move the door to the Farallon Islands," it relieved tension in both the audience and the speaker, breaking down the wall of formality that had been inhibiting communication. Humor helped to ease audience resistance and get the point across while keeping tensions under control.

But humor was even more valuable in dealing with the question-and-answer session. The audience would become unmistakably hostile at times, hardly listening to the officers' earnest answers. The captain gave me a short list of the most common angry questions he faced during the sessions and I was able to provide him with the comic ammunition he needed to defend himself. When asked, "Why is 911 always busy?" he replied, "You're right, the 911 number has been getting a greater volume of calls than we anticipated. In fact, we're thinking of changing the number to 7-11 because *they're* open 24 hours a day." In response to "What can a small business owner do to protect himself against crime?" he answered, "Never leave your partner alone with the safe!" He would of course follow these with his serious explanations—to which the audience was considerably more receptive than they had been in the past.

A real-life ad-lib from an SFPD patrolman illustrates this even better. Two officers were called on one of the most potentially dangerous situations police can face— a domestic squabble. As they approached the apartment building where the disturbance was taking place, a television set came flying out of a third floor window and crashed to the sidewalk at their feet. They rushed upstairs and knocked on the door. "Who is it?!" a voice inside roared out. "TV repairman," came the reply.

Many business leaders use the same technique. When Don Kendall was president of Pepsico, he was put in what could have been a very awkward position when a reporter asked him how he could justify his salary of

$800,000 a year. Kendall replied, "I have a wife." While this may have offended some women in the audience (not a policy I recommend), it effectively got Kendall out of a tight spot.

Shortly after the breakup of AT & T, I worked with phone company speakers to create humorous material for the many public appearances at which they would try and explain the reorganization. When asked why long-distance rates were continuing to rise, the answer was: "It's true that long-distance rates are going up—that's the bad news. The good news is . . . the continents are drifting closer together."

Sometimes a joke can simply change the pace of a serious presentation and allow the audience—and the speaker—to remove themselves from the situation, refocus, and see things in a different light. This is especially valuable when the audience has prejudged your topic as boring or otherwise unpleasant. Remember, in the old days they killed the bearer of bad news! Today we still tend to mix up the message with the messenger. Using humor may not change the news, but it will help take the sting out of it, and perhaps allow people to better put it in perspective. At a regional sales presentation that recapped an off year, one corporate vice president broke up the low-key meeting by announcing: "We've had a bad year, but so have a lot of other people. After all, Gary Hart was caught with more than his sales down!"

Of course, a funny answer must always be followed by the real answer, or you'll appear to be just a wise guy dismissing the question. And while the truth may still hurt, at least the audience will be listening. The sales manager mentioned above followed up her joke with the hard facts, telling the audience: "Our situation was not quite that embarrassing—but here are the figures. . . ."

Humor Makes the Memory Grow Fonder

As the above examples have shown, humor can be very useful in setting up a serious point, or in illustrating or dramatizing an idea. It paints a verbal picture (a cartoon, really) that's more graphic and easier to remember than mere words. It's also an effective way to advance the general theme of your speech. Walter Mondale made good use of the popular commercial catch phrase "Where's the beef?" in promoting his argument that his Democratic primary opponent (you know who) lacked a substantial campaign platform.

Humor is similarly valuable in summing up a message in a clear-cut way, especially when you're trying to sell someone on an idea rather than just transmit information—as when candidate Ronald Reagan proclaimed: "Recession is when your neighbor loses his job. Depression is when you lose your job. Recovery is when Jimmy Carter loses his job."

Humor Makes Your Audience More Willing to Listen

People don't generally like to be preached to—they will always prefer a joke to a sermon. So when you're trying to instruct or inform your listeners, humor can be a valuable teaching aid. Humor implies a certain insight, perceptiveness, and (dare I say) intelligence. Since the audience is more apt to respect a witty speaker, they'll also be more willing to listen to what you have to say.

A rather interesting study supports this point. A group of high school students were asked to rate their teachers on a scale of one to five according to teaching ability and also to the humor level in the classroom—how often the class laughed and how often the teacher made humorous comments. Out of the 284 teachers rated, those ranked at the top in teaching ability averaged 3.95 on the humor scale. Those judged to be the poorest teachers averaged 2.36 on humor. While this may not be conclusive evidence of anything, it seems to show that humor is more often characteristic of a good teacher than of a poor one. And since speakers—and executives in general—often present an image of a teacher by their example and their authoritative position, the study appears to support what we said right at the beginning: A sense of humor makes a valuable contribution to effective leadership.

By the way, did I tell you about my favorite teacher in college? On the first day of class he said to a large lecture hall, "For the next hour I'm going to talk, and hopefully you're going to listen. If you should finish before I do, please let me know."

Humor Should Mean Fun—Not Fear

If our most influential and respected leaders are not afraid to use humor in their most important presentations, why then is everyone else so reluctant? Perhaps the seriousness of the Protestant work ethic is engrained too deeply in the heart of the American business person. Playing the fool is not consistent with attaining power and success. Sound plausible? Yes—but it's not true. I discovered this early in my career as a corporate humor consultant. I had, against my better judgement, agreed to present a workshop on the "effective use of humor in business communications" at an annual conference of a Big Eight accounting firm. My slot was to be part of a three-day program featuring numerous seminars and workshops from which participants could choose ones to attend. I was hoping desperately that I would at least get enough people to hold the class without being embarrassed. Blue-suited, white-shirted accountants did not seem to me to be the type that would go actively seeking enlightenment in the ways of humor.

Then, two days before the conference, I received a call from the executive who had arranged for my presentation. I felt sure he was calling to cancel, and I actually felt relieved that I would not have to face a too-small group. It was quite a shock when he asked me if I would mind doing two sessions, in order to accommodate all those who wanted to attend! The room, he explained, only held 60 people.

I ended up doing the two sessions to packed rooms. And while they were all wearing white shirts and blue suits, they were one of the most receptive, inquisitive groups I've ever spoken to on humor. They really did want to know how to be funnier. They had simply never known how.

Over the years, I've consistently heard executives say, "I'd really like to use humor, but . . ." (pick one or more):

1. I don't know how to fit it into my speeches.

2. I don't know where to find humorous material.

3. I'm just no good at telling jokes.

4. I'm no comedian.

5. I'm afraid I'll look foolish if I fail.

This book will soon eliminate fears #1, #2, and #3. Consequently, #5 will not apply (and anyway, it's much worse to be DULL than to tell an unfunny story). As for #4: Let me now reveal to you one of the most important points to be made in the book, a point I will elaborate on in a later chapter. It's simply this: You don't have to be a natural comedian to use humor effectively in a business setting. What's more, as we'll discuss in Chapter 3, the business speaker who uses humor has a great advantage over the professional comedian.

After the fear of using humor has been eliminated, there may still remain some skepticism about the average person's ability to create his or her own material. There should not be. Writing comedy is not the mysterious, murky art that many people believe it to be, at least not at our level. Creating humor for a business presentation is not quite the same as writing jokes for Johnny Carson's nightly monologue, or scripting a blockbuster movie comedy. Anyone with a sense of humor can create jokes for a speaking presentation—using many of the same formulas employed by professional comedy writers.

That's right, I said formulas. There are some very structured, time-tested ways of writing jokes, and they're relatively simple to learn. Creating funny material can be as easy as applying your natural sense of humor to a basic set of rules. But there is a still-easier technique used by professionals that you can also learn. It's a method that allows you to to turn old jokes into new ones, create many jokes from a single idea, and most importantly, turn inappropriate or irrelevant jokes into humor you can use. This magical, simple technique is called "switching," and you'll learn all about it in Chapter 4.

How to make irrelevant jokes appropriate may well be the most important thing you'll learn about using humor in business. A joke that is appropriate for your audience and your subject does not need to be terrifically funny to get a positive reaction. If you're able to deliver it with an air of self-assuredness, failure is next to impossible.

And that is what this book will emphasize throughout: the key to a speaker's effectiveness lies in selecting humor that is appropriate and delivering it with confidence. Of course, do this keeping in mind the words of Noel Coward: "Wit ought to be a glorious treat, like caviar; never spread it about like marmalade." It's that simple.

Humor Is Good for You, Too

You've no doubt heard about publisher Norman Cousins's experience with "the healing power of humor," but I believe it's worth repeating briefly here to make a point. Cousins was suffering from a degenerative spinal condition brought on by a type of endocrine imbalance that can be caused by tension and frustration. His doctors gave him 500 to 1 odds against recovery. But Cousins had other ideas. He wondered if, since negative emotions had damaged the endocrine system, perhaps positive feelings—like laughter—could repair it. Moving from a hospital to a hotel room, Cousins barricaded himself in with humor: "Candid Camera" tapes, Marx Brothers movies, and other funny stuff. And it worked. Within a few years he was completely cured.

So I ask you: If humor can cure a hopelessly degenerative disease, couldn't it make your speech a little better?

CHAPTER 2

All Jokes Are Not Created Equal

Selecting Appropriate Humor

This chapter shows how to select humor that is appropriate for your audience and your subject matter. It also illustrates how to:

➢ Slant humor to fit a particular audience
➢ Know who and what are safe to make jokes about
➢ Sense the mood of an audience
➢ Use self-effacing humor effectively
➢ Match humor to your subject or situation
➢ Fit humor into the right places in your presentation
➢ Begin a joke without disrupting the flow of your speech
➢ Use humor effectively when you must emcee a program of speakers or events

The chapter also discusses the relative merits of several different easy-access sources of humor.

➣ ➣ ➣

What do we mean by appropriate humor? Here's an illustration: Myron Cohen, one of the great comic storytellers, once told of a true-life incident that happened to him in Boston. He had been booked for a week-long run in a popular local nightclub. On the last night of his engagement, however, the club had been previously reserved by a local Irish-American organization, the St. Joseph's Guild. Although the club owner did not say anything to Cohen, Myron knew that the man would have much preferred to replace him on that night with a popular local comic, Jimmy Joyce—who was often called "the Irish Myron Cohen. " Cohen approached the clubowner to reassure him and told him there was no need to worry, he would do just fine with the St. Joseph's Guild. Although the other man was skeptical, he was too honorable to break his commitment to Cohen, and agreed to have him perform as scheduled. When Myron took the stage that night, the first thing he said was, "Good evening ladies and gentlemen. My name is Myron Cohen . . . but I'm often called the Jewish Jimmy Joyce. " The audience roared their approval, and were with him all the rest of the night.

Being a top professional, Myron Cohen knew the value of *involving* the audience by tailoring a remark specifically to them. Perhaps there were some in the audience who were at first wondering, "Why couldn't they get Jimmy Joyce?" Cohen addressed exactly what was on their minds—in a funny way—and won them over.

You can learn to do the same, simply by doing the two things professionals do: *personalize* and *localize.* These techniques are both aspects of *slanting,* or tailoring humor to fit your audience or your message. The first part of this chapter will concentrate on slanting humor to your audience, including how to choose the target of a joke and how to best use self-effacing humor. Then we'll discuss making humor appropriate to your subject and your situation. We'll next talk about pacing, or when and where in your speech to use humor. Finally, we'll review some sources—where to find humor.

Mirror, Mirror: Slanting Humor to Fit the Audience

As Jimmy Durante used to say, "Everybody wants ta get inta the act." It's true: people love to be recognized as being special, unique individuals. That's why it benefits you as a speaker to tailor material to involve a specific audience. When you do this, you tell your listeners, "I'm one of you. I share your understanding of things." It implies that you also share their concerns—and breaks down that persistent barrier between speaker and audience.

You'll see examples of this whenever you see a professional comic work. When Bob Hope was performing to enlisted men at military bases around the world, he would never fail to include some remark about the commanding officer, or the food, or some other subject with which those particular soldiers were well acquainted. Most nightclub comics will single out someone in their audience and ask, "What's your name? Bill? Bill, where are you from?" Later on in the act, the comedian will inevitably return to that person, even if simply in an aside after a joke ("Isn't that right, Bill?"). Bill breaks up, and the rest of the audience loves it, because one of their number is *recognized*. When I was performing in San Francisco in the early 1980s, and the 49ers were pro football's dominant team, all it took for a comic to win a roar of wild approval from an audience was to get up and say, "How about those 'Niners?" Using the names of local teams, people, streets, restaurants, and the like impresses an audience no end. Some scorn this as a "cheap laugh," but that's usually because they didn't think of it first.

Who Is the Audience?

Tailoring material to an audience is not always that simple to do. A good business speaker must often research his audience a little to find out what's on their minds. The more you know about a group, the easier it will be to get laughs from them. When I'm asked to write funny corporate material, I always have a lot of questions to ask before I can begin to work on the assignment.

First of all, what's the situation? Is it a sales conference, or a convention, or a roast? Is it being held on the premises, or at a "fun" outside location? Is the audience familiar with the location, or have they never been there before? Is it an in-house presentation, or will there be outsiders involved?

But the most important question is, *who* is the audience? It's critical to be aware of what the audience has in common if you expect to win them with "in-jokes." My favorite target is a group's common enemy or competitor. Politicians do this almost exclusively when they use humor: they joke about Republicans to Democratic audiences, about liberals when addressing conservative audiences, and so forth. But this technique is even more impressive when you zero in on a particular business. I once did a humor job for a West Coast representative of a certain Mexican beer, who was making his semiannual presentation aimed at exhorting the local distributors on to greater sales. He was particularly concerned about a competing Mexican beer that was beginning to take away some of their market. Few other audiences would have fully appreciated the joke when he told them: "People always say don't drink the water in Mexico. Well, they've been doing something about it. They bottle the water now. They call it [competing beer's name]."

Know What's Hot — and What's Not

It's also helpful to know what the current hot topic of conversation is among the audience. It might be the newest technical development in their field, or simply the current office gossip. It could be they're all talking about the firm's latest and greatest accomplishment, or they may be complaining about something that's affected them all in a negative way. Make absolutely sure, however, if you joke about a group's complaint, that it's something *they* see the humor in and joke about themselves. If a subject seems at all like something the audience could be sensitive about, check it out first with someone who knows for sure.

For example, a joke about airline safety should probably be avoided if you're talking to a group of air traffic controllers or pilots. Even though both these groups may often be vociferous in their complaints about safety problems, they don't want to hear others taking pot shots at something so important to them.

One comedian friend of mine made a similar kind of error in judgement when he performed for a group of IRS employees (as a favor to a friend!). He assumed that they wouldn't mind the kind of jokes that the general public loved, so he opened with: "This is the first time I've been in a room with people from the IRS and not had to pay to get out!"

This remark might seem like harmless fun to you or me, but to this audience, it represented more of the same kind of put-down they'd been hearing for years. To further aggravate the effect, a local newspaper had run a somewhat uncomplimentary story about them earlier in the week. They groaned and immediately turned off to the comic, and it wasn't until he was well into his "regular" (non-IRS) material that he finally won them back.

At a more basic level, it's also important to have an idea of the audience's degree of intelligence and their areas of interest. If you're going to joke about something topical, make sure your listeners read the papers or watch TV. Your witty barb about baseball players' salaries will be lost on an audience that doesn't follow sports.

It all comes down to knowing what the audience wants to hear and saying it funny—in their language. Learn what they're thinking and either say it or show you know it. People like to be approved of. And they certainly don't want a speaker to make them angry. For instance, most civic organizations, service clubs, and business associations tend to be politically conservative. They're against higher taxes, big government, and liberal court systems. You don't need to compromise your principles if you disagree—just don't tell them what they *don't* want to hear. Always avoid making fun of the audience or their beliefs—no matter how funny they may seem to you! Don't do what President Franklin D. Roosevelt did when he opened an address to the ultraconservative Daughters of the American Revolution (DAR) with the words, "Fellow immigrants. . . ."

Vive la Différence! Male and Female Audiences

One of the most often overlooked factors in the make-up of an audience is also one of the most important to a speaker: Is the audience mainly men or women? There are some major differences in the sexes' reactions to humor. Women laugh more easily than men. Okay, I don't have any scientific studies to back me up on this, but I'm basing my statement on years of experience, observation, and the concurring opinions of other professionals. Most pros will agree that an all-male audience can often be the hardest to make laugh, while an all-female group is the easiest. And it has nothing to do with relative sense of humor. It's much less complicated than that.

Humor, successfully used, confers power or control over an audience. We must "let our guard down" to laugh. If we laugh too hard we become "helpless" or "weak" with laughter. In our society, men are conditioned to avoid this at all costs. They are more reluctant to laugh than women, perhaps because they have been conditioned to *avoid* appearing weak, helpless, or just plain silly. Think about it—tough guys never laugh (except maybe when they're pouring a few slugs into another tough guy). This fear of foolery becomes magnified when they are surrounded by other men. Who wants to be the first to let his guard down? It's just not macho.

This is why, when facing an all-male audience, it's especially important to make sure you joke about something that's of common interest, so that you bond yourself to the audience—kind of become one of the guys, right? If it's not a homogeneous group of men in the same company or the same field, the locker-room standbys are generally a good bet: sports, business, or—women.

How to Do It

Now that you know what to do, let's look at the techniques professionals use to slant their material. Right up front, let me tell you that the most important element of slanting is truth. You must make the jokes believable— up to a point. Think about how a joke works. It's largely based around the element of a surprise. You lead the listener down the garden path, and at the last minute—you trip him up. But he doesn't care, because by then he's laughing! He followed you until it was too late to turn back.

To accomplish this trickery, you must embellish your joke with factual details that the audience can easily understand and relate to. This means filling in around the punch line with names of people, places, and things they know. For example, always specify the location of the joke. Never just say, ". . . a street in a large city." Make it ". . . over on Wilshire Boulevard" (if you happen to be in Los Angeles). Instead of "Two men were talking," it should be "Joe Smith, your sales manager, and I were talking yesterday." Don't say "I went into a store," but rather "I was in Macy's" or whatever the local retailer is.

It often helps to use a little audience participation when setting up a joke. Don't be afraid to ask a friendly question or two, like "Have any of you ever been there?" after mentioning a place, or "Have any of you ever done that?" And what better way to get audience sympathy and identification than by asking, "Has that/this ever happened to you?"

When doing jokes about something currently in the news, always ask who's heard about it or read it in the paper (a favorite technique of Johnny Carson). This question can't lose: either they've heard about it and will feel on common ground with you, or they haven't heard about it, and will pay more attention to find out what they missed.

When You Don't Have All the Background Information

The specific changes you make to the lead-in or "setup" of the joke are, of course, dependent on the particular audience, occasion, and situation. Sometimes you may not know specific place names or people, but that shouldn't stop you. The idea is simply to change the characters and other details in the joke over to things the listeners will identify with.

For example, I laughed when I first heard this old New York garment-center joke:

A man rushed into a clothing store and said to the owner, "I understand my son has owed you for a suit now for the past year and a half." "That's right," said the other man hopefully. "Have you come to settle the account?" "No," he answered. "I wanted to buy one on the same terms."

This is a pretty funny joke one might want to use, say, when speaking to a group of—computer programmers? Watch:

An executive went into a computer store and said to the owner, "I understand my office manager has owed you for a computer system. . . ."

How about with a group of carpenters?

A foreman went into a hardware store and said, "I understand one of my carpenters has owed you for a set of tools. . . ."

As you can see, it's possible to allow almost any group to identify with your material if it's slanted right.

The Truth Will Make You Funny

When you talk about yourself while getting into a joke (or make yourself the subject of the joke—a good idea we'll discuss shortly), use true facts from your own life. If you're not married, don't joke about a spouse. If you do have children, mention them—or mention your dog, or your car, or your cab ride from the airport, or anything that's real. Before you can expect to draw the audience in, you must believe your own joke—you will sound much more convincing if you do. You want them to believe that your story actually happened to you. Share something truly personal with the audience and they'll accept you more easily. *Then* you can pull the rug out from under them—and they'll love it.

I was able to do this once after experiencing a very rough flight into San Francisco. I told my audience all about it—the choppy ride, the turbulence, the nervous passengers (including myself!), the sudden dips that caused the flight attendants to lurch down the aisle. Since everyone had been in that situation at one time or another, they all knew I was being completely truthful. And since it really did happen to me, it was easy to sound convincing. Then I added, "But I really knew we were in trouble right after dinner. Instead of serving coffee, they gave everyone a life jacket and a rabbit's foot." My audience, completely taken in up to that point, burst into laughter that probably would not have been nearly as great if the joke had been told out of context.

Choose Your Target Carefully

When you mention real people in your joke—such as a coworker or anyone known personally by those in the audience—it's generally a good idea not to put them down in any way. On the contrary, take the opportunity to boost them. Make them seem like important individuals, whether they are or not. Let the audience know that this person is accepted by his or her peers and respected by you.

For example, one company held a small ceremony to honor their building's maintenance man when he retired after many years of service spent sweeping their floors and emptying their ashtrays. He was widely known in the building for his highly polished bald head—but to make fun of him for this would have been unthinkable. Instead, the speaker turned what could have been an unkind put-down into a warm compliment, saying: "God made lots of heads—those he was ashamed of he covered with hair."

There are times, however, when it may be appropriate to make a real person the target, or butt, of the joke. After all, *someone* has to be. (Even in the gentle joke above, people with hair are actually the target.) In every joke, someone or something has to take the fall, so to speak, so that everyone else can feel superior and laugh. There is one simple, ironclad rule to follow when selecting the butt of the joke: Make sure you choose a big enough target. Everyone takes shots at the phone company, or the Pentagon, because these massive institutions are basically immune to the ill effects of harsh words. If sticks and stones don't break their bones, mere words will do less than nothing!

Bob Hope has made fun of U.S. presidents for years and everyone, including each of the presidents, has loved it. A big target is generally flattered that he or she is big enough to be singled out. Some of you of the right age group may remember a very popular TV show of the mid sixties, "The Soupy Sales Show." Soupy personally brought back pie-in-the-face comedy for a while, as he would take one in the kisser on almost every show. As the show became more popular, he added a unique twist: Celebrities began to appear on the show, expressly for the honor of being hit with a pie. Everyone who was any-one at the time eventually appeared—even Frank Sina-tra! It became a badge of honor among the famous to have been hit in the face with a shaving-cream pie. The implications of this still boggle the mind (*my* mind, anyway). More recently, Don Rickles and Joan Rivers come to mind as those who bestow high honor on the rich and famous by insulting them.

Now consider this in a business context. Everyone likes to laugh at the boss, and the boss doesn't have to wor-ry—because when the laughter stops, the boss is *still* the boss. Those in power generally love this kind of recog-nition from subordinates, because it only serves to rein-force the fact that they *are* subordinates. But what if the situation is reversed? How do people feel when the boss makes fun of his secretary in front of the other employ-ees? Often, it then appears that the big boss is picking on the poor little underling—something very few of us find amusing. Never attack a small target. People have a natural tendency to sympathize with the underdog. And as basketball's Wilt Chamberlain once observed, "Nobody roots for Goliath."

How Not to Do It: The Inappropriate Supervisor

Many years ago, I witnessed firsthand how damaging this kind of mistargeted humor can be. A manager I worked with considered himself something of a wit, and unfortunately, his favorite target was his hard-working secretary. It seemed that anything she said or did was 'fuel for "humorous" insults from the boss.

When she mentioned she was going to the ballet, he cracked (loudly) "Ahh . . . you just wanna see those men running around in tutus!"

When she wore different clothes to work, his comment was: "Someday they'll be in style . . . or come back in style."

At a meeting when she tried to explain something and became flustered, saying "I've lost my train of thought," he jovially remarked: "I didn't know you had one." Naturally, any suggestions she made at any time were referred to as "another one of your off-the-wall ideas."

When other employees began coming to her defense and telling the manager to lay off, he replied, "It's just my sense of humor." Finally the secretary couldn't stand it anymore and confronted him. She said simply: "I don't think your remarks are funny, and no one else does either. If you have any real criticism of me you should tell me directly and privately." The manager was stunned. He had had no idea of the effect his "sense of humor" was having—but everyone else did, and thought it rude and inappropriate. He stopped making jokes about his employees.

Avoid Sexist, Ethnic, and Religious Targets

While we're on the subject of what's not an appropriate target, let's say a word about sexist/ethnic/religious jokes: No. Any remark that denigrates a particular race, religion, gender, or sexual preference will eventually get a speaker in trouble. This is because, no matter how non-malicious the intent may really be, you can be sure *someone* will always be offended. When dealing with volatile material, it's impossible to predict how everyone will react. And even if the joke gets a laugh, it may leave an uneasy negative impression about you in the back of people's minds. No one is really comfortable with a speaker who attacks these kinds of targets. If you're trying to get people to like you, it makes sense to use material that makes a listener proud—not embarrassed—to be a member of a particular group.

Humor as Social Commentary: Handle with Care

It is possible, of course, to use humor to point out prejudice, injustice, and the general foolishness of humankind—people have been doing this for centuries. There is a famous old story from the World War II era about a socialite who wanted to treat some soldiers to a home-cooked Thanksgiving dinner. She called the nearby army base, spoke to one of the first sergeants, and asked that three soldiers be sent to her house that Thursday. But she also said, "And Sergeant, I do not wish any of them to be Jewish." The sergeant said, "I understand, ma'am." On Thanksgiving day, the woman answered her door to find three black soldiers waiting. "We're here for Thanksgiving dinner, ma'am," said one. The shocked woman sputtered, "But . . . your sergeant must have made a mistake." The soldier said, "No ma'am, that's impossible. Sergeant Cohen doesn't make mistakes."

Although you may not see what could possibly be wrong with this story, beware. As I said, you simply cannot predict how an audience will react—believe me, they can misunderstand *anything*. It's safer not to use this type of story in a business setting. Better to leave the social commentary to Mort Sahl and other professionals.

When I was performing stand-up comedy in San Francisco, I had a rather strange experience that convinced me of just how unpredictable audiences can be in the way they interpret jokes. It was shortly after President Reagan had appointed Sandra Day O'Connor as the first woman justice on the Supreme Court. I did a line on it that was hardly worth the trouble it caused me. I said, "The only reason Reagan appointed a woman was because he thought he could save some money on her salary." Okay, it's not the funniest joke, but it made a timely point, didn't it? Unfortunately, just what the point was has been open to question. The audience began to boo and hiss. Aha, you say. Don't joke about Reagan to a bunch of his supporters, right? Yes, but this club was in the heart of the Haight-Ashbury section of San Francisco, possibly the world's strongest remaining bastion of old hippies, liberal politics, and anti-Reaganism.

But the audience didn't care that the joke was a jibe at the president whom they all opposed. They didn't hear that. All they heard was a remark that put down *women*—and it set off a knee-jerk response. People have a way of reacting emotionally when they even *think* that they or their values have been attacked. Don't put them in that position.

What Do You Mean, We?

A very common error in judgement occurs when a speaker believes that simply because he or she is a member of a particular ethnic group, it's okay to tell a joke that denigrates that group. This may be all right in a one-to-one situation where you know the other person, but as we saw above, in a crowd there's always someone who'll be offended.

When I was a young boy I accompanied my Italian grandfather to a Knights of Columbus meeting in our largely Italian New York neighborhood. The K of C was a totally homogeneous group, and the featured speaker was also of Italian descent. Yet this didn't help him when he began his talk with a rather questionable story: "I was almost late getting here. You see, I locked my keys in my car. But fortunately, I'm a graduate of Italian driving school. The first thing they teach you is how to open a car door with a bent coat hanger."

This was met with some uncomfortable grumbling. A few people groaned, a few laughed politely, but the majority of the room sat in stony silence. And another ethnic comic went down in flames.

If there's any chance that the joke may alienate a portion of the crowd, it's foolish to use it. In other words, stay away from sexist, ethnic, and religious targets.

Have a Good Day? Get a Sense of Audience Mood

Of course, a target that's wrong for an audience may not always be so obvious. Often it's necessary to try and be aware of a particular audience's mood—particularly when dealing with jokes on current events. Even the most sensitive subjects in the news can generally be joked about after they've had time to cool off. Jay Leno's crack about the weirdo who had been tampering with Tylenol—"This must be the same guy who's going around to the restaurants switching the real coffee for Folger's instant" —got big laughs after sufficient time had passed since the tragic deaths. If you're not sure whether an audience is still going to be touchy about a topic, you should just stay away from it. If it's still in the news every day, don't even *think* about it.

A comedy writer/comedian friend of mine, Tom Finnigan, actually had a joke taken away from him for a while because of public feeling about a current event. Since shortly after the 1980 presidential election, he had been getting good laughs (from Northern California audiences) with the line: "President Reagan will never get assassinated . . . because everyone who owns a gun *voted* for him." Of course, after the president was shot, that joke had to be filed away for some time. It emerged much later as, "I was really surprised that someone tried to shoot President Reagan. . . ."

By contrast, Bob Hope covered the same subject from a different angle and got away with it while the president was still recovering: "President Reagan is in the hospital telling one joke after another. The theory is that the bullet passed through Henny Youngman." Bob Hope, however, can get away with this—for a number of reasons. He's perceived as a friend of Reagan. It's always seen as okay to make fun of someone if you're a member of his in-group. But just let someone else try it, and watch out! Also, Hope has made a career of making fun of all the presidents under all kinds of circumstances. It's expected of him. We'll talk about this phenomenon at length in the next chapter.

Even Hope, however, is not totally immune from a hostile public reaction. I will not repeat his infamous joke about AIDS and the Statue of Liberty (I try to *learn* from mistakes). Suffice it to say that Bob and his writers underestimated the sensitivity of the public to that very frightening issue. And if they can turn on Bob Hope, just think about the treatment the average speaker might receive when he steps beyond the bounds of good taste. I don't believe it's worth the risk.

Roasts: How Low Can You Go?

There are certain situations, however, where insult humor is expected and, in fact, welcomed. These events are called "roasts," and at one time or another, almost everyone gets a chance to be a roaster or roastee. Roasts are becoming more and more popular as an alternative to traditional awards or retirement presentations—because they're just more *fun*. Often, however, feelings are hurt because the humor crosses that fine line between fun and meanness. This can result in embarrassment for the roastee, the roasters, and everyone else who must sit through it.

I once attended the retirement roast of a man who was known within the company to have a serious drinking problem. The audience sat in shock as one of the man's fellow employees used every drunk joke in the book (not this book, of course): "We didn't know what to get him, because we didn't know how to wrap up a saloon. . . . He reminds you of the old saying, 'Where there's a swill, there's a way.' . . . He's never joined Alcoholics Anonymous because he's never sober enough to remember the pledge."

These may be okay if you're roasting someone who's known to occasionally have a drink after work. Then it would be obvious that the jokes were tremendous exaggerations of reality. But it only works if everyone knows that he's not really a lush. The most important thing to remember about roasts is that you must keep the humor to things that are obviously untrue—and then make it more obvious by exaggerating.

The safest thing to do is to keep your remarks to the unimportant things that can't be embarrassing or damaging in any way. For example, on one company roast I wrote for, the organizer gave me just that kind of information on the people to be roasted, such as:

JIM: Smokes like a fiend. Favorite color—and everything he owns—is brown.
FRED: A golfing fanatic, but a terrible golfer.
MIKE: Drives 80 mph all the time. Scary driver.

These are ideal things to joke about because they don't reflect personal problems and are basically unimportant in relation to each person's character and job performance. No one gets embarrassed—and everyone has fun. Oh, the jokes?

JIM: What can you say about a guy who smokes three packs of cigarettes a day? Well, he's got a heart of gold . . . and fingertips of brown.
FRED: He's hit so many balls in the water, the fish are going to start charging him green fees.
MIKE: People kid him about his driving, but Mike told me that when he first went for his license, he got 18 out of 20 on the test. Two guys were able to get out of the way.

Make Yourself the Fall Guy

There is one target that is always appropriate as the butt of the joke with any audience: You. "Never set yourself up as being superior to the audience," comic Jay Leno has said. This is particularly true for the business speaker. You should never lead the audience to believe you're better than they are socially, financially, or intellectually—because if you're an upper-level executive or even a frontline manager talking to employees, you may well be better off! You want the audience to accept you as one of them—or perhaps even let them feel superior to you in some small way. That's why self-effacing humor is so effective.

Rodney Dangerfield has made a very successful career of telling people, "I don't get no respect." When Rodney first began to get recognition in the late 1960s, the great Jack Benny remarked that Dangerfield's comic "character" (a concept we'll discuss in detail in Chapter 3) was the best he'd ever heard of. It was perfect, said Benny, because "*no one* gets respect."

It's true. And misery loves company, right? People love to know that someone else suffers as badly—or even worse!—as they do. It comforts them to see their own faults reflected in another person, especially one who seems to be in a position of power—like a speaker. An audience also likes the fact that you're openly admitting your weaknesses, whereas they don't have to. They can sit back and feel safe in their self-esteem while they laugh at you. But although they'll laugh, their respect for you will not diminish. On the contrary, they'll respect you more, because they'll see that you're self-confident and secure enough in your position to joke about yourself. After all, look at some of the other people who do just that:

At the 100th anniversary meeting of the American Bar Association, guest speaker President Reagan remarked, "It's not true that I attended your *first* meeting."

When President and Mrs. Kennedy traveled to Europe and she got all the attention from the French press, JFK introduced himself to reporters by saying, "I am the man who accompanied Jacqueline Kennedy to Paris."

An executive client of mine was speaking to a group who did not know him well. He was on a program, however, that featured several other speakers who were widely recognized by this audience. His opening comment was, "Most of the speakers you'll hear today constitute a sort of who's who in the industry. I'm more in the category of who's *he*."

Whenever you're altering the details of a joke to suit an audience, always try to change it so that you're the target. If it's a joke about someone who has something bad happen to him or her, or does something foolish, substitute yourself for the person in the joke. Not only will it make the joke more believable (and therefore funnier), but the audience will appreciate you more even after the laughter has died down.

Tailor Humor to the Subject/Situation at Hand

In addition to tailoring humor to fit a particular audience, effective speakers also make humorous material relevant to their topic or to the situation they're in. There are two ways to do this: *directly*, in the subject matter of the joke; or *indirectly*, in the point that the joke makes.

Making a joke directly relevant is easy enough to understand. If the situation you're in happens to be a banquet, a joke about the food usually goes over well—especially if the food didn't. One client of mine opened his after-dinner speech by saying, "I hope you all enjoyed your dinner as much as I did. I'm no cook, but I don't think leg of lamb is supposed to glow in the dark."

Similarly, if your topic is real estate, jokes directly about houses and property values make sense. I once did a writing job for a client who conducted seminars on how to profit from buying and selling foreclosure property. For a part of his talk, he told of all the work that went into restoring badly rundown houses to salable condition. When he described his own experience with his first ramshackle house, he got the audience's attention by telling them, "That house was in such bad shape, the termites called it junk food."

It Adds up to Laughs: Humor Helps Facts and Figures Come Across

When you have to present a lot of figures—for sales or production, for example—an appropriate joke is especially valuable in holding your audience's attention. Large numbers often become meaningless to people, particularly when they're faced with a series of them in a short time. A joke that illustrates what the number means would be perfect, but even a line that simply pokes fun at the number or statistic will be welcomed by most listeners. One of my most unique clients, a tugboat company executive, did this when talking about the increasing cost of fuel: "The cost of fuel has gone up to $308 per metric ton—and they won't even wipe off your windshield."

I inserted a similar line into the speech of an oil company executive who was talking about the size of certain holdings: ". . . 68 million acres—or approximately the size of the Ewing ranch" ("Dallas" was TV's number one show at the time).

These jokes don't realistically illustrate a point, but they definitely make dry statistics a lot more palatable. The listeners may not remember a $308 million or 68 million acre figure, but they'll have a memorable point of reference to call to mind that the speaker was saying *expensive* or *big*.

One-liners such as these don't necessarily need to make a point. They serve to make a positive impression with your audience, showing them that you don't take your subject (and by implication, yourself) too seriously and that you have things in the proper perspective. They also give your audience a little break without letting their minds wander too far. A long joke, however, might lose the audience unless it has something to say that will carry your message forward. So generally, when you're joking directly about your subject or situation, it's best to stick to a short one-liner.

Use a Longer Joke to Make a Point: The Indirect Approach

The longer, story-type joke is usually more effective when you want to make an important point—indirectly—that you want to leave with the audience. Parables have been used to teach people for thousands of years for the same reason certain jokes stick around that long—they work. Try to think of your stories in the same terms: you are trying to illustrate a point, clarify it, make it more vivid, more memorable—and more persuasive. The subject of your story need not be directly related to your message as long as the meaning is relevant—although ideally you'd like to have both when possible.

A joke that makes a point will always be more likely to get a good response than one that is told just to get a laugh, for obvious reasons. It will meet with less resistance from the audience, because they will appreciate that the speaker is *primarily* trying to make a point. And even if they don't find the story particularly funny, they will still tend to accept it as long as it communicates a message. Another advantage of a meaningful joke is that you don't have to worry about whether it's too old or familiar. An old joke can be very useful in helping to get something across to an audience if it's used in a new way. And as we'll soon see, there are many, many ways you can make a single joke illustrate a number of points—you're only limited by your own imagination.

There's a simple three-step technique for using a story to illustrate a point. It's similar to that standard speaker's process of "Tell 'em what you're gonna say, say it, and tell 'em what you said." For humor it's just slightly different: (1) State your point; (2) tell the joke that illustrates the point; (3) restate the point.

A client of mine who was trying to downplay the importance of statistics did it like this:

Statistics can be dangerously misleading. I remember when my grandfather turned 97 years old, and I asked him if he ever worried about dying. He told me he thought his chances were slim, because he looked in the obituaries every day, and very seldom did he find people over 97 dying. [pause] Yes, statistics can be easily misinterpreted.

While this makes the point about statistics, it could very well be open to a different interpretation if used in another context. Suppose he was speaking to a group of older Americans, trying to convince them to stay active? Or if someone was speaking on any variation of the power of positive thinking or some other motivational theme? Almost every good joke is loaded with possibilities for a variety of meanings, if you look beyond the surface.

One of my favorite old jokes is one sometimes known as "the airplane joke." It's a simple good news/bad news bit:

The pilot of an airplane got on the intercom while the plane was over the Pacific Ocean and said, "Attention, passengers. I've got some good news and some bad news.

The bad news is, we're totally lost and I have no idea where we are. The good news is, we're way ahead of schedule."

This joke has been around for many years (the airplane was probably a covered wagon in the original version). While it's funny enough, it's not exactly a real killer. It is, however, laden with meaning—if you want it to be. In my time I've heard it used to make a number of points, including the following:

1. You must be goal-oriented to get anywhere.

2. Plan ahead.

3. Effective leadership is essential.

4. Every cloud has a silver lining.

5. Incompetent personnel will lose customers.

Get the idea? All it takes is some thought and a little imagination. Here's another joke that's open to interpretation. Study it and see what you can come up with before looking at my list.

Three stores on the main street in town were located right next to each other. One day the store on the left put a sign in the window that said SALE—ROCK BOTTOM PRICES. The next day the store on the right put up a sign that said SALE—LOWEST PRICES IN TOWN. The next day the manager of the store in the middle put up his sign: MAIN ENTRANCE.

Now think about it for a moment. Never mind specific points for now—just consider some of the themes you might be speaking on that could be illustrated by this story:

1. Competition

2. Advertising

3. Marketing

4. Creativity in business

5. Creative problem solving

6. Business ethics

7. Necessity is the mother of invention.

Try adding your own themes or subjects to this list, and then come up with a specific point that the joke makes regarding each one.

Consider All Factors When Deciding What's Appropriate

Here's a little exercise in joke selection. The speaker in this situation is a real estate professional talking to other real estate salespeople. The topic is "Trends in Real Estate for the 1980s." Let's look at four jokes that might be used during the presentation and decide which one is the most appropriate—and why.

1. These days when someone pays in cash it arouses suspicion. People think his credit is no good.

2. You know the three biggest lies in real estate: you can refinance in a year; the house only needs minor repairs; and you can afford the balloon payment when it comes due.

3. One buyer told me, "I always wanted to write something that would last forever. Who knew it would happen when I signed a mortgage?"

4. Many first-time buyers find it hard to qualify. It's un-

fortunate for everyone that the person who writes those bank commercials isn't the same one who approves the loans.

Number 1 makes me laugh, but it's really too far removed from the subject—and from reality. While one's credit rating is relevant to buying real estate, the connection needs to be made more directly. It's stretching it to base a joke on someone paying cash for real estate (how many people actually do that?).

Number 2 would be nice if you were talking to a roomful of potential buyers, since they could probably relate to hearing those very statements from enthusiastic salespeople. But in this case it insults the audience. "Lies"? Would you call your audience a bunch of liars?

Number 3 is another that would be more appropriate for an audience of customers rather than sellers. Since it pokes fun at the buyer's predicament, it actually denigrates the real estate profession somewhat, telling the audience, "Look at this poor sap and the mess we've gotten him into."

Number 4, on the other hand, sympathizes with the customer (reassuring the agents that they are indeed a sympathetic lot) and attacks a common enemy—the banker who won't lend people money (so deserving realtors can make some money of their own). Its subject is right on point and quite familiar to the audience, and the joke attacks the right target. It's a good joke for this speaker.

Let's look at another example, this time where the speaker is not talking to his peers but to a group of potential customers. Suppose the speaker is a financial planner who's giving a free seminar to attract new clients. The audience is a mixed group of people who are considering using the services of the speaker. Which of the following would be most appropriate?

1. I know of one financial planner whose luck was so bad, his portfolio dropped 50 percent in one day . . . and this was a Saturday.
2. With my own investments, I sleep like a baby—all night I sleep an hour, then wake up and cry for an hour.
3. There's only one sure-fire method for getting a small fortune out of the stock market: go in with a large fortune.

Number 1 makes the mistake of putting down the competition—and consequently, the profession in general—to a group of outsiders. Barbs against the competition work best when you're talking to a homogenous group of their business rivals. Then the competition is a common enemy to rally against. The general public (and your potential customers) might simply feel this is a cheap shot on your part against someone who's not there to defend himself.

Number 2 is self-deprecating—which is generally a good idea. But in this case it's not. If you're trying to inspire confidence in your professional abilities, don't give the audience any reason to doubt it (such as by their thinking "Hmm . . . they say there's a grain of truth in things said in jest"). Again, this would be more appropriate if one were talking to a group of peers—who didn't need to be convinced of the speaker's professional competence.

Number 3 is the best choice. It says what many skeptics in the audience may already be thinking. Therefore, it establishes the speaker as an honest, up-front kind of person—just the type you'd want to do business with.

Pacing Yourself

An often-overlooked aspect of the appropriate use of humor is *pacing*, or *when* to use humor. The proper placement of jokes in a presentation is critical. Many speakers seem to feel it's enough to open with a good joke and then play it straight the rest of the speech— and lose the audience along the way. Some speakers go overboard, peppering the entire presentation with jokes and in the process burying their actual message or information. The audience comes away smiling, but wondering what it was really all about.

At the risk of sounding overly simplistic, I'd say that humor should be used in three general areas of the speech: at the opening, interspersed throughout the body of the talk, and (you guessed it) at the end. But there's more to it than that.

Humor at the Start Opens the Door

Humor at the beginning of a presentation breaks down that initial atmosphere of formality between the speaker and the listeners. Nonhumorous openings often sound stilted. The audience is nervous anyway, wondering if they're going to agree with the speaker or even like him at all. A clever remark right at the start helps them decide. Audiences *want* to like you. When they see that you have a sense of humor, they begin to make all sorts of positive assumptions about you: you're witty, warm, self-confident, intelligent. If they feel they've got a handle on what kind of a person you are, they'll be more willing to listen to what you've got to say.

Since this first impression is so important, you should pay careful attention to the kind of joke you select for an opening line. It should be broad and not too tough to figure out. An obscure reference that may not be picked up by everyone right away should be avoided. You want the audience to *know* you're joking. Remember, they're probably not expecting humor at this point. More subtle jokes are okay later on, when listeners have realized you're not going to be as dead serious (and deadly boring) as other speakers they may be accustomed to. But up front you must *clearly* let them know that you are going to be pleasantly different.

An opening joke should never include references that assume a great deal of specific knowledge—of any kind— by the audience. I was amazed at hearing one seminar leader open his presentation with a joke that referred to dinosaurs! The punch line, fortunately, escapes me now. The confusion it generated managed to increase initial tensions and keep the audience uneasy well into the first part of the seminar. Have *you* heard any good Tyrannosaurus Rex jokes lately?

Another reason to take special care in selecting that first joke is because it characterizes you for the audience. In other words, if your first joke is in some way offensive, your listeners will assume, "Oh . . . he does *that* kind of humor." And if your opening is simply not funny, your listeners may just tune you out immediately. In humor, as in life, first impressions are lasting impressions.

This point was brought home to a comedian friend of mine who actually had one of the cleanest acts of any night club comic I've ever heard: no four-letter words, no overtly sexual jokes, no bathroom humor. He did, however, have one joke of questionable taste that he unfortunately used as an opener: "I'm a little upset tonight . . . my wife just had a breast removed. Now she's got two like everyone else."

This one poorly placed bit of bad taste came back to haunt him later on when he was rejected for a local television appearance because, according to the producer who had seen him, "His act is too dirty. He does that joke about the breast and stuff." There was no other "stuff" in the act remotely like it. But it didn't matter—he was categorized on that opening line.

The ideal opening is a good personalized/localized kind of joke. It immediately tells the audience that you're really interested in them. They'll appreciate that you've singled out a reference they're especially familiar with and will likely be on your side from the outset. The Myron Cohen opening referred to at the beginning of this chapter ("My name is Myron Cohen, but I'm often called the Jewish Jimmy Joyce") is a perfect example of a good personalized opening line.

A speaker at an Atlantic City convention tuned in to his locale when he opened by saying: "It's great to be back here in Atlantic City. I have to be careful, though. Last year I got a little bit out of control and gambled away my car . . . and boy, was the guy from the rental agency mad!"

Ease into Your Opening Line: Lead-Ins You Can Use

Many speakers are unsure about how to start off a joke. Actually, it's probably easiest to do at the beginning of a speech. If we keep in mind that all humorous comments should sound like things that really happened, then the three types of lead-ins discussed in the following paragraphs make sense:

The "on my way over here" lead-in. This is a traditional show business opener, and in that context it's a cliché.

But in a business situation, when the audience is not thinking in those terms and the element of surprise is still on the speaker's side, it can be very effective. I usually recommend starting with "It's nice to be here . . ." and then "On the flight into town . . ." or "At the airport . . ." or "Driving in this morning . . ." or other variations on this. The key to making it work, of course, is to personalize and localize.

When I spoke at a conference in suburban Chicago, I began by telling the audience about my cab ride from the city. "It's good to be here in one piece . . . I had an exciting cab ride from the city. When we got here I asked the driver what his average tip was for this trip. He said, 'Five dollars.' So I gave him five dollars and I said, 'Gee, you must do all right driving a cab in this town.' He said, 'Not really. This is the first average tip I've gotten this week.' "

Now, this might be construed by some as a put-down of the city's cab drivers, but actually, the nastier the cabbie, the prouder city folks are of them. Take it from me, a native New Yorker. *Our* cabbies make the ones in Chicago look like drivers' ed instructors.

The "I was talking with . . ." lead-in. Mentioning a conversation with someone known to the audience (like the emcee, the chairman, or the boss), or a conversation overheard, is another effective way to get into a joke right at the top. One of my favorites was used by a writer friend of mine who gave a talk to a local writers' group in San Francisco. "When I first talked to John Kent [the organizer of the group] about coming here, he offered me a small honorarium. When I declined it, he was very happy—he said he would put the money into the improvement fund. I asked him what that was and he said, 'We're hoping to save enough money so that next time we can have a better speaker.' "

This is especially good because it's slightly self-deprecating—always a nice touch. This type of lead-in can also be used effectively pretty much anytime in a speech, since a conversation you had or overheard can usually be tied in to any point or subject covered. Just be sure to use relevant people in a relevant place.

The subject lead-in. A very straightforward way of opening that also works well is to immediately tell listeners what you will be talking about, and then joke about it. A marketing seminar leader speaking in New York City did this with an excellent localized remark. "Marketing is not an easy subject to explain," he said. "Trying to figure out what the public will want is like trying to guess when George Steinbrenner will fire a Yankee manager." The reference to the New York Yankees' volatile owner was perfect for the Manhattan audience, and they roared their approval (and acceptance of the speaker).

Keep Them Awake: Intersperse Your Speech with Humor

While the humorous opening is by far most important in connecting yourself to your listeners, you shouldn't stop there. Unfortunately, I've heard a lot of speakers do this. They begin with a nice funny remark or story, and then that's it. Very often the audience— which started out alert and hopeful—fades away halfway through the presentation. To avoid this, you should use humor throughout the speech to hold (or bring back) their attention. Let's face it—audiences don't listen to very much of any presentation. They tune out quickly, often slipping into daydreams without realizing it. If you intersperse your entire presentation with humor, listeners stay a little more alert, not knowing when they're going to be surprised with something funny. It also works as a change of pace to regain the attention of those who may have already turned you off. The bottom line is that you'll have a better chance of getting your serious message across because they'll be listening a greater percentage of the time.

Although you should make an effort to space jokes as evenly as possible throughout the speech, always remember that your primary consideration must be appropriateness. Sometimes it's simply impossible to make a joke fit correctly in an arbitrary spot. I've had clients tell me they wanted "one joke on each page of the speech." This is ideally the right approach, but realistically it's important to just use good judgement about how many jokes should be used and exactly where they should go. There is no one correct answer to the oft-asked question, "How much humor should I put into a serious speech?" As usual, you must consider the nature of your subject and audience in deciding how to approach each presentation. And always keep in mind the basic purposes of humor before you position it anywhere in a presentation: does it help to make a point or to hold the audience's attention?

Some speakers have a problem finding the jokes they put into the body of their speech when they are actually up at the podium. Humor blended into the written text sometimes tends to sneak up on the speaker—the speaker doesn't notice the joke until he or she finds himself or herself telling it. In such cases jokes may be delivered simply as if they were an ordinary part of the presentation. As we'll learn in Chapter 3, this is a very ineffective way to tell a joke! To avoid having your humor surprise you in the middle of a speech, it's a good idea to highlight the jokes on the page or index card with a yellow marker. When you come to that part, you'll notice immediately what's coming up, and you'll be prepared to give the joke the emphasis it deserves.

Leave 'Em Laughing

This is another show business cliché that holds true for business speakers as well. The right closing joke can leave a memorable impression on an audience and help drive your message home. A concluding joke, then, should always reinforce your theme or your most important point. I enjoyed the very neat ending to a speech by a woman who owned her own Silicon Valley computer firm. She was speaking to a group of new women MBAs and had talked about her own triumphs and difficulties as a female entrepreneur. She concluded by saying, "The people in my company joke that I'm the token woman in the office. That was my way of meeting the EEO requirements—I hired myself as president. I hope each of you will have the chance to do the same."

I heard another wonderful conclusion to a speech by a corporate VP who was speaking on the importance of good customer service. It was tied in to a company-wide campaign stressing this issue, and his closing summed up his message perfectly: "Being customer oriented should be inseparable from producing a quality product. There's no point in maintaining high production standards if we can't follow through with quality at the point of sale. It's like the man who went into a very exclusive Beverly Hills clothing store to buy a suit. The salesman asked him for his name, occupation, hobbies, educational background, religion, and political party. The customer said, 'But all I want is a suit.' The salesman said, 'Sir, we don't merely sell you a suit. We make a suit that's exactly right for you. We analyze your personality and your background. We search the world for the kind of sheep that produces just the wool your character and mood require. The wool is processed according to a special formula that reflects your personality. Then it's woven in a part of the world where the climate is most favorable to your temperament. Then, after a series of preliminary fittings, we style a suit. But then. . . . ' 'Wait a minute,' the customer said. 'I need this suit for a wedding tomorrow afternoon.' The saleman shrugged and said, 'Okay, you'll have it.' "

When You're the Emcee

Pacing becomes particularly important when you're the one who must conduct an entire program of different presentations. Whether you're called the emcee (MC, for Master of Ceremonies), chairperson, or program coordinator, your role is essentially the same: keep the show moving and don't get in the way. There are two simple elements involved in accomplishing this.

Be tactful. This is the main character requirement of a good emcee. It's your job to build interest in the other speakers on the program. You mustn't "take over" and upstage the others or subordinate them to yourself, so be brief—use one-liners, don't tell stories. Don't talk too much about the speaker's subject—leave that to him. And of course, don't insult or embarrass anyone that you don't know well—no matter how mild or how funny you think your insult may be.

Get the audience in the right mood. Even more so than when you're a featured speaker, you must be sensitive to the mood of the crowd. As emcee, you must bear the brunt of any of their negative feelings and try to turn them around. If they're quiet or bored, you need to come on lively and upbeat. If they're wild and boisterous, you may have to calm things down. It's up to you to set the tone of the program and to make it as easy as possible for the other speakers.

In order to get a handle on the type of audience to expect—so that you can decide what kind of humor will be appropriate to use—consider the speakers and the purpose of the program. An annual employee talent show, a sales conference, and a political rally will draw vastly different crowds, but each should have its own homogeneous qualities. By doing a little of the research discussed earlier, you can come up with a fairly accurate portrait of your listeners in time to prepare for them.

We'll learn more about how to deal with different types of audiences in the next chapter. For now, just know that to be the perfect emcee, all you have to do is keep the program going smoothly and don't be obtrusive.

Where to Find It: Sources of Humor

Although many business speakers complain that good jokes are hard to find, there are many sources of seemingly uninspired material that can be made to work. Most of it appears at first glance to be unfunny and unusable—but these jokes are really diamonds in the rough. Later in this book you'll learn how to polish them into humorous gems, so consider them now as valuable raw material.

Magazines. For decades, Reader's Digest has told us that "Life in These United States" can be funny. And they've proved it with a wealth of humorous fillers in every issue. Not all of them are funny, but again, they're a source of raw material and ideas—and some of them *are* funny and may be appropriate as is.

In addition to popular magazines and daily newspapers, trade publications can also be useful, especially for specific humor particular to that business. If you're speaking to a group from one industry, try to get hold of a trade journal or in-house publication. These are often the best sources for "inside joke" material.

Whenever taking a joke from any publication, use an old copy—at least a year old. If it's been recently published, chances are your audience will recognize both the joke and the source—which, while not disasterous, is usually embarrassing. Try the public library or your dentist's office for old back issues.

TV or other speakers. In show business, it's called stealing—a grievous sin. On the speaking circuit, it's simply recycling good material. Don't be afraid to "borrow" something that another speaker has gotten a laugh with—because he probably borrowed it from someone else!

If you hear something funny from a comedian appearing on TV or in the dialogue of a sitcom, write it down. With only slight adaptations, these jokes can work as perfectly in your presentation as they did on national television. As with magazine jokes, stay away from very recent things. If you heard it on a popular TV show last night, 20 million other people are probably familiar with it by now. The thing to do is watch reruns of shows like "M.A.S.H.," "All in the Family," and "Taxi" —all great sources of top notch one-liners (that most people have by now forgotten).

You should also avoid popular jokes currently "going around." Countless speakers have been embarrassed after telling the great new joke they just heard and then discovering that everyone else heard it (several times) last week. Even worse is when someone has told the same joke earlier in the same program.

A largely untapped source of excellent jokes that I like is comedy records and tapes—the old ones, of course. Many of the comedians we see today only in the movies and television—like Woody Allen, Bill Cosby, and Bob Newhart—were brilliant young stand-up comics 20-odd years ago, and fortunately, their nightclub acts have been recorded for posterity. You may have to do some hard searches of record stores and garage sales, but it's well worth it—for your own enjoyment, if nothing else.

Cartoons. Many of the most popular newspaper comic strips are simply illustrated one-liners. I'm not talking about social commentary like "Doonesbury" or "Bloom County." I'm talking "Garfield," "The Wizard of Id," "B. C.," and the like—the strips that use basic setup/punch line action in four or five panels. Sometimes the jokes are pretty good. Sometimes they're pretty adaptable. Even if you don't find anything usable, you may get some good ideas.

Joke books. The main complaints people have about jokebooks is that the jokes are usually dated, and they're not funny anyway. Very often this is true (not in this book, of course). Still, bad jokes are just the raw material we mentioned earlier—material you'll soon learn to shape to fit your needs.

Joke services. A joke service is a sort of "joke periodical." It's usually a monthly (or sometimes weekly) newsletter-type collection, largely made up of very current topical jokes. Since the writers of these services must regularly produce **x** number of jokes for each new issue, a lot of it is not so funny—but at least it's not dated. Joke services are used quite a bit by radio personalities who need a steady supply of on-air patter. One legendary former San Francisco deejay, "Dr." Don Rose, was said to have con-current subscriptions to 14 different services! The cost is usually in the area of $100 per year (I've seen them as low as $40 and as high as $200). If you're not in radio, I can't see why you should need to subscribe to a joke service, but if you can afford the luxury, I guess it couldn't hurt.

Comedy writers. Hiring a pro to write your humorous material gives you the advantage of getting it (or at least asking for it) made to order for your presentation. You must often pay dearly for such service. The real problem, however, is finding a writer you can work with. Besides the usual personality clashes involved in the typical writer-performer relationship, you have the added difficulty of finding a funny writer who knows (or can learn) your business-related subject matter. Too often, familiarity with the business world and a sense of humor do not appear in the same writer. If you *really* feel you must work with a writer, call me—I'll be in the San Francisco or Marin County (California) telephone directory.

Writing your own. Chapters 4 and 5 of this book will give you the necessary skills to handle all the joke writing you'll ever need. Try it before you turn anywhere else.

Keep a File

I strongly recommend keeping a file of the jokes you find funny. Even if a joke doesn't appear usable right now, save it anyway. At some point you may be in a situation where it is appropriate—a good, funny joke will always come in handy *sometime*. The file should be alphabetized according to subject, and cross-referenced as much as possible.

For example, suppose you're filing the "three stores" joke used earlier in this chapter. Ideally, it should be filed under, say, Competition, and cross-referenced under Creativity, Advertising, Marketing, and so forth. I can't tell you how many times cross-referencing has saved the day for me. A humor file is not nearly as useful without it.

You can keep your file on traditional 3 x 5 index cards in a showbox, on 5 x 8 cards in a Rolodex, or if you're a "techie," on your computer. With a computer you could create a "file" for each subject. You would then be able to easily call up all the jokes on any subject—and you don't have to alphabetize anything!

A CHECKLIST FOR CHAPTER 2

Research the audience.

Choose your targets carefully.

Avoid sex, race, and religion.

Be aware of the mood of the audience.

Use self-deprecating humor whenever possible.

Use longer stories only to make a point.

Open and close with humor—and pace yourself throughout.

CHAPTER 3

Delivering Humor with Style

This chapter covers every aspect of delivering humor effectively, including:

➢ How to go about developing your natural sense of humor into a comic personality at the podium
➢ A variety of tips for improving presentation skills
➢ Examples of "safe," low-risk humor you can use instead of jokes
➢ Suggestions on how to develop comic timing
➢ What to do if the audience doesn't laugh
➢ How to make humor seem spontaneous—including 33 "ad-libs" you can use in unexpected situations

➢   ➢   ➢

Several years ago, I stood in the back of a San Francisco comedy club and watched helplessly as a novice comedian was torn to shreds (not literally, although it might have been preferable) by a hostile crowd. The newcomer stumbled through his material, pausing tentatively every so often to listen for laughs that never came. In place of laughter, the audience offered astute observations like, "You stink—get off the stage!" and "When does the comedian come on?" and "What is this—a dramatic reading?" The patron in front of me probably summed it up best when he grumbled, all too loudly, "I paid five bucks to get in here. When's this jerk gonna be funny?"

That, as they say, is show business. Nightclub audiences are often like predatory animals—they can smell fear. When the victim—er, the person on stage—shows the slightest hesitation, they move in for the kill. Take my word for it: it is not a comforting thought to realize, when standing there and looking out over the lights at those unsmiling Mount Rushmores, that what they are collectively saying to you is, "Okay, mister funny guy— make me laugh."

Now contrast this with another kind of public speaking situation—the kind that's supposed to be more serious. When President John F. Kennedy took office in 1961, he brought an entirely new dimension to that dry and often predictable affair known as the presidential press conference. Reporters had been conditioned over the years to expect a staid question-and-answer session, and had little reason to anticipate anything different from the 35th president of the United States. Imagine their surprise and delight the first time someone asked a question like, "Mr. President, when do you think this country will put a man on the moon?" and JFK replied, "Whenever Senator Goldwater wants to go." Time after time, an audience anticipating the usual litany of standard responses was treated to an unexpected display of wit.

And they appreciated it so much that the serious answer which inevitably followed was also better appreciated.

President Kennedy took advantage of his audience's not-so-great expectations. Taken out of context, his clever remarks were not in themselves uproariously funny, but the president knew what every witty speaker knows—you don't *have* to be a comedian.

Consider your typical business presentation. People have attended this sales meeting or convention or training class simply because they need the information you have to offer. They don't care if it's entertaining—they probably don't expect it to be. After all, the cheerless informational meeting has become a staple of American business. The greatest expectation many people have in this kind of situation is simply that when it's over, they'll wake up refreshed!

And this is what gives you a tremendous advantage over the stand-up comic. Your listeners are not demanding that you make them laugh. Their expectations are much lower than they are for the comedian, because they perceive you as being there to deliver a basically serious message. If you choose to throw in a touch of humor, the audience is usually so relieved (if not *grateful*) that they're more than willing to give you a chuckle in return. And that's all you really need—a chuckle, not a belly laugh. Many speakers seem to believe that if they make a humorous remark, it's a failure if it's not met with riotous laughter. Wrong. For the comedian, laughs are a goal. For the business speaker it's merely a means to an end. Your purpose in using humor, remember, is merely to put your audience at ease, create rapport, and get your serious message across more effectively. If you happen to get a big laugh, fine—but that's not your ultimate purpose in a business situation.

Use Humor That's Appropriate for Your Personality

Many speakers wonder about what type of humor works best: one-liners, stories, personal anecdotes, or even sight gags. The answer is simple: all of them—or none of them. It depends entirely on who's delivering the material. In other words, *be sure to use humor that fits your speaking style.* Rodney Dangerfield would not be funny using Richard Pryor's material. Lee Iacocca would not be effective using Ronald Reagan's material. Every good speaker or humorist develops his or her own way of getting a message across.

The importance of creating a distinctive personal brand of humor is often overlooked by the nonprofessional speaker. A recognizable individual style, or *comic persona,* can in fact be more important than the jokes one delivers. It will carry weak material, getting laughs out of *how* the speaker says things rather than what he says.

Remember the classic routine of the late Jack Benny? A gunman approaches him and says, "Your money or your life!" After a *long* pause, Jack replies, "I'm thinking, I'm thinking." This got laughs for decades because of Benny's firmly established "tightwad" personality. Without that comic character to carry it, the joke doesn't work nearly as well—if it works at all.

A writer for Bob Hope told the story of sitting in the audience during one of the comedian's performances in England. Hope delivered a joke in which the word "motel" was critical to the punch line. Since the word is not commonly used in England—they call them hotels and inns, but never motels—the writer was surprised to hear the audience laugh heartily at this joke they probably didn't get. He turned to the woman next to him and asked why she was laughing. "Because he's Bob Hope and I know he's funny."

A more telling example of the power of style came in the early days of stage comedy. The great Al Jolson, to prove a point to a friend, went out and delivered four jokes minus the punch lines. He would build up the gag to the end and simply stop short; and each time, the audience laughed anyway—because he was Jolson.

I'm not saying that you have to become an internationally famous humorist to make an audience laugh. The point is that the speaker who has developed a consistent, distinctive style of humor that audiences can quickly recognize will have a tremendous advantage over one who has not. He or she will be less dependent on sharp material and better able to get laughs by just being himself or herself—which is always the ideal to strive for.

It's not easy. Even Woody Allen has admitted that, in his stand-up comic days, he at first thought that all he had to do was get up on stage and recite funny material. Not surprisingly, his early nightclub performances were less than completely successful (he once turned his back on the audience and finished his act talking to the wall behind the stage). But like every other successful comic before and since, he discovered that he had to learn to *perform* his lines and create a comic *character* out of his natural personality. To a slightly lesser degree, the business speaker must do the same.

How Will I Find Myself If I Don't Know Who I Am?

How does one begin to find a personal style? By considering all the possibilities. Some people feel comfortable telling long stories, while others have too much trouble remembering them. Some enjoy firing off one-liners, while still others are embarrassed by the idea. More importantly, what is the "attitude" of your humor? Is it angry, self-effacing, politically aware, dumb? You may have to experiment with different types of things to find the best method of expressing your sense of humor, but rest assured that after a few "experiments" it will all become clear. Think about the comics you enjoy. You probably tend to reflect (distortedly, of course) something of their styles when you joke around with friends in relaxed situations. That's okay, if you add a touch of your own personality. Ask yourself two simple questions about your own comic personality: (1) What is my point of view? (2) How do I express it? When selecting jokes to use, always consider these questions and select material that reflects your attitude.

If you study some of today's popular comedians, you'll see that each has a very firmly established comic character. Consider how certain comics would answer the above questions:

Johnny Carson, the observer of current events:
His point of view is that, upon examination, the news of the day is rather absurd. He expresses his point of view by making caustic, funny comments about what's happening.

Rodney Dangerfield, the loser:
His point of view is that the world is out to get him and nothing ever goes right. He expresses this by complaining angrily about everything that happens to him, as in "I don't get no respect."

Don Rickles, the insult comic:
His point of view is that in some way everyone is a jerk and needs to be told. He expresses it with direct, rapid-

fire insults aimed at his audience, celebrities, and people in general.

Sometimes the same comedic point of view can be expressed very differently, resulting in an entirely different type of character. Woody Allen, like Dangerfield, has always been identified with the "loser" persona. While his point of view is essentially the same as Rodney's, he expresses it in a completely different way. Instead of fuming about "no respect," his character simply resigns himself to bad fortune, reporting it matter-of-factly—with just an occasional wimper.

Similarly, Joan Rivers has become something of an insult comic like Don Rickles. But while her point of view is the same, she expresses it differently, confining her insults to the famous and making the audience a confidant rather than a target.

When you find the style of humor that suits you, polish and perfect it—and stop your experimenting. It's crucial to keep a consistent comic point of view. In other words, don't try to be a political satirist one day and a self-effacing "hard luck" type the next time out. Don't worry, your real personality—or the one you wish to project—will shine through on certain kinds of jokes more easily than on others. And of course, the audience will help you decide what works best for you.

The Hidden You . . . An Improvement on the Original?

A comic persona can actually take a lot of pressure off of you. When you develop a distinct style, the character often takes over, and ad libs come naturally. A San Francisco comedian friend of mine was shocked to discover this for himself. Larry had a basically low-key, self-deprecating stage persona, and it worked well as an extension of his true personality. But he had high standards when writing his material, and sometimes found it a real chore to come up with a steady supply. Then he discovered "Bobby."

Like all of us, Larry had more than one side. Within that low-key guy was hidden (or repressed) a more outgoing (though still bitter), "Vegas" kind of guy. He took to occasionally trying out that personality on stage—doing an entire set in the "Bobby" character—and was startled by the results. Larry's uptight, highly structured act had suddenly become a relaxed display of off-the-cuff remarks, with new material developing right on stage. "I'm amazed at some of the stuff I've come up with as 'Bobby,'" he now says. Experimenting was obviously worth the risk in this case.

Sometimes character develops by accident. Earlier I referred to Jack Benny's trademark "tightwad" persona. It came about in a very typical fashion. Once, on one of Benny's early radio programs, he did a "cheap" joke that got laughs. Since it worked the first time, the writers gave him a couple more for the next week's show. These also got laughs, so they threw in a few more for the next show, and the next, and the rest, as they say, is history. The audience knows best. Listen to them.

No Pun Intended—Please!

Now a word of caution. Some people are fond of puns. I have found most of these people to be painfully unfunny. As you may well know, puns and word plays will most often elicit a groan. If there is laughter, it is given up grudgingly. This is because, by its very nature, a pun is a statement of how clever one is—how much more clever than the audience! The speaker is in effect saying, "Look at me, I thought of this cute word play, aren't I smart?"

The purpose of podium humor is to make the audience *relate* to the speaker and accept him as one of their own. A pun has the opposite effect: the audience is made to feel they're supposed to be impressed with the speaker's scintillating wit. Puns have no place in effective business humor. Save them for use between consenting adults in the privacy of your own home.

Safe Humor: Someone Else's Words Will Never Hurt You

There are, of course, people who feel uncomfortable telling any kind of joke. If you are one of these faint-hearted types, there is still a low-risk choice of humor you can use: quote someone else who is known to your audience. This is a very safe way to go because it takes the pressure completely off of you—after all, if they don't laugh, it wasn't *your* line that bombed!

For example, one executive responded to a question about his projected budget for the coming year with a remark by one of history's most respected (and witty) statesmen: "As Winston Churchill said, 'I always avoid prophesying beforehand—it is a much better policy to prophesy after the event has already taken place.'"

One client of mine opened a speech to a farm group with Mark Twain's classic definition: "A banker is someone who lends you an umbrella when the sun is shining, but wants it back when it starts to rain."

Lines like this may not have audiences rolling in the aisles, but remember, they're not supposed to. They do serve the purpose of giving a light touch to an otherwise solemn occasion—and with minimal fear of embarrassment for the speaker.

Compared to What?

Another kind of humor that's fairly safe to use is the humorous analogy. This is essentially a funny comparison, identifiable by its use of the word "like" as in the remark by a Silicon Valley computer analyst who had just taken over his first managerial position: "I feel like the bridegroom on his wedding night. He knows what he has to do—the question is, can he deliver?" Here's one from a financial planner's presentation that needs no explanation: "Paying a financial consultant $100,000 a year to manage a personal portfolio is like hiring Billy Martin to manage the company softball team."

When in Doubt, Leave It Out

If you have any doubts about the humor you've selected to use, *leave it out.* I cannot stress this enough. If you deliver humorous material with anything less than complete confidence, you're asking for trouble. It's a simple fact of comedy life that if you don't think your material is funny, you can rest assured that the audience will not think so, either. As baseball's Jim Wohlford once said, "Half of this game is 90 percent mental."

Longer Should Be Funnier

If you discover you are the story-telling type, keep in mind another important rule: *The longer the joke, the funnier it will have to be.* As I said in Chapter 2, a story that makes a point will be much more likely to at least get a polite laugh. But when you spend several minutes building up to a punch line, the audience expects a big payoff. If they don't get one, you'll find yourself with the proverbial (or perhaps actual) egg on your face, listening to a long, loud groan. A dud of a one-liner can be easily glossed over—remember, just keep talking—but when a story dies there is a pause that cries out to be filled, and generally it's filled with the speaker's embarrassment. To avoid this, stick to stories that are time-tested—that means you've personally heard them get laughs. Always test out a story on someone (or several people) before using it in public, just to make sure you're not the only one who thinks it's funny.

With some long story jokes, it's especially advisable to be funny "on the way" to the punch line. In other words, throw in a few one-liners while building up the story. This is most important when the story is a little too hard to really believe, or when it's obvious the audience knows it's not true, or when it's simply very long. I don't generally recommend telling jokes like these, but if you happen to have a five-minute shaggy dog story that you simply must tell, get them chuckling well before the punch line.

Always Try It Out First

It's important to test out material on friends before using it at the podium. An obvious benefit of testing a joke is that it gives you an opportunity to practice your delivery in front of an audience. This gives you a chance to get really comfortable with the material. You should play with the phrasing, timing, and word emphasis, and compare people's reactions until you find just the right way to say it—that is, the way that most consistently gets laughs. Even an audience of one or two can help you decide whether to revise or polish your delivery. Study people's reactions carefully. Are they bored? The joke's probably too long. Do they look puzzled? You may have told it too fast (assuming that it is basically funny).

Try it out on as many people as you can in as many settings as you can: one on one, in small groups, at parties, at work, and on all kinds of people. And learn to distinguish the polite laugh from the real one. Remember, most people don't want to hurt your feelings, so they'll pretend to laugh at almost anything.

There are no set rules for deciding just who you should practice on. The more people you try, the better you'll be able to judge your material.

One rule of thumb might be drawn from Woody Allen's opinion on the subject of breaking in new material for a nightclub act. While most comics that I've known tended to try out the new stuff before sparse crowds on "off" nights at a club (the theory being that it will be less painful to bomb this way if the material doesn't work), Allen believed just the opposite. He felt that it was better to try new material in front of a boisterous packed house than in front of a late-night group of a few hangers-on. With a weak crowd, he reasoned, it's hard enough to get laughs with your best material—so you're not really giving the new stuff a fair chance. If, on the other hand, it bombs with a lively crowd that's laughing at everything else, you can be pretty sure that it's no good.

However, a business speaker shouldn't be afraid to try out a joke on someone who's known to be a real "sourpuss." There are bound to be a few in any audience, anyway, so you're going to have to face them sooner or later. If he or she laughs, you know you've got a good joke, right? By the same token, there are some people who'll truly laugh at anything. Don't be misled! These types are not as often found in business audiences, so don't depend on their reactions as a true gauge of what's going to work for you.

Whenever you try out a joke on someone, *don't* tell them you're testing it for future use and would like their opinion. Everyone loves to give their opinion on what's funny and how it could be made funnier. You don't need someone to listen critically and then give you an analysis; you simply want them to react emotionally. Catch them unawares when an appropriate opportunity arises and spring the joke on them. If enough people laugh, it's funny. Nothing could be simpler.

Keep It Conversational

Still another good reason to test out a joke—or at least say it aloud to yourself—is to make sure that the joke is in *conversational language*. There are many jokes that may read funny in a joke book, but sound stilted and decidedly unfunny when you attempt to repeat them as they were written. Change the wording a little so that it fits your normal way of speaking. For instance, drop those unnecessary adverbs the joke books are so fond of. You know, in phrases like ". . . she said sweetly" and ". . . he said with obvious glee." Eliminate and replace any words you don't normally use when speaking. Does anyone say "desist" instead of "stop"? "Advised" instead of "told"? Remember, you're supposed to be talking to a group of new friends.

If the story involves dialogue between characters and you're uncomfortable about altering your voice for each one, don't. If you just turn your head from side to side when repeating dialogue, the audience will easily be able to distinguish who's talking to whom. But don't forget to change it from the written ". . . he growled" or ". . . she purred" kind of language to a simple "he [or she] said."

Finally, *always* cut down the number of words. Jokes are a lot like poetry: you want to get a maximum impact from a minimum of words. One of the best examples of this was also one of the most funny/sad newspaper headlines I have ever read. When New York City was going bankrupt, and then-President Ford refused to allow the federal government to bail them out, the New York Post headline concisely reported, FORD TO CITY: DROP DEAD.

Make Sure the Punch Line Is at the End

Whenever you alter the wording of a joke, try not to rearrange the punch line too much. For example, here's a little test. What's wrong with this joke?

When I was in the hospital, the board of directors sent me a telegram and, by a vote of five to four, wished me a speedy recovery.

It's not a bad joke, is it? But something is not quite right. It's awkward. That's because the key phrase, the *punch line*, is not at the end. What makes this joke funny is the phrase, "by a vote of five to four." To put "wished me a speedy recovery" at the end takes away from the impact of the joke. Always keep in mind that the basic idea of delivering humor is to build suspense and end with a surprise:

When I was in the hospital, the board of directors sent me a telegram and wished me a speedy recovery . . . by a vote of five to four.

Timing Is Crucial

Note the three dots (. . .) before the punch line above. In comedy shorthand, this means *pause*. Which brings us to our next point: Always *pause* before the punch line and *wait* for the laugh afterward. You need only pause for a second or two. That's enough to provide the audience with a subtle cue to get ready to laugh. The pause gives them the time to visualize the verbal picture you've created, or simply to grasp the situation you've described. Professional comedians call this *timing*, and old-timers like Bob Hope and George Burns are masters of this art. The next time one of them is on television, listen with an ear for timing and you'll find that the laughs come from what they say and how they say it, but also from those moments when they say nothing at all. "Timing is not so much knowing when to speak," said Jack Benny, "but knowing when to pause."

While it takes years to perfect one's timing, it's fairly simple to learn the mechanics of it. In fact, most good one-liners have the pause built in. One former client of mine who was under fire for certain activities faced a hostile group of reporters with the opening line, "Ladies and gentlemen of the press, I have considerable respect for your tolerance in inviting me to address you . . . and for my courage in accepting." When you know where the punch line is, it's easy to find the natural place to pause.

By the way, it's called a *punch* line for a reason. When you deliver it, don't just say it in the exact same tone of voice as the setup. Lean into the mike and really *punch* it out. Or at least change your tone enough to distinguish these crucial words from the rest of the joke. Think of the punch line as almost a separate part of the joke, and rehearse saying it louder and clearer. If the audience doesn't quite catch what you said, they're not going to laugh.

After delivering your punch line, you face a true test of courage: you must wait for the laugh. The natural instinct is to rush ahead to the next thing you're going to say, but this often serves to "step on" the laugh and defuse the effect of the joke. The pause becomes a test of fortitude because that space of a few seconds between the time you deliver the punch line and the time the laughter arrives can truly seem like an eternity, as your ego hangs in the balance, waiting for the audience's decision.

Don't attempt to fill the void by laughing at your own joke. Nothing sounds more pathetic than the solitary laughter of an unsuccessful joke teller. Even when the audience does laugh, it's generally poor form to join in yourself. Better to act mildly surprised, and let the audience feel that they discovered the joke you didn't quite realize was so funny. Remember, the audience will like you better when they can in some subtle way feel superior.

If you study top professionals, you'll see that they all have little quirks that cue the audience to laugh after a punch line. George Burns will take a puff of his cigar. Joan Rivers will nod and vigorously point a finger around the room. Bob Hope or Johnny Carson will simply stare straight at the audience. These gestures all announce that, "You've just heard a joke and it's okay to laugh now."

Of course, if that laughter never does come, you'll realize why they call it "dying." But have faith. If you've paid attention to the rules up to this point, the laughter *will* come. So give the audience time to respond—and be aware that not everyone will start and finish laughing at exactly the same moment.

But What If They Don't Laugh?

So what should you do if a joke falls completely flat? Nothing. Just keep on talking! You've got a better chance of pretending it never happened than you do of "saving" it with a follow-up comment ("What is this, an audi-

ence or an oil painting?") that will only call attention to
the fact that your remark was unappreciated. Leave the
"savers" for the pros. They work for Johnny Carson on
"The Tonight Show" because he *is* Johnny Carson *on*
"The Tonight Show."

Even if they really don't like the joke, even if they *groan*
at it, at least it serves to give them a breather from your
serious message. A little break like this gives the audience a chance to mentally refresh themselves and get
ready to listen again. And whatever happens, don't start
making on-the-spot revisions in your planned material
if the first joke or two doesn't work! This means you
shouldn't drop, add, or change any of the humor you
were going to use, or you'll end up destroying all the
careful preparation you put into it (and if you *haven't*
prepared carefully, you're probably getting what you
deserve). If you find your material isn't working and
needs changes, work them out later, in the safety of your
home or office—*not* at the podium.

Another good reason not to "bail out" (comedian talk
for deliberately giving up early) on your material is this:
It only takes one good laugh line to turn an audience
around and get them with you for the rest of the way. I've
personally seen (and experienced) this many times. Often
the audience may not get the idea that they're supposed
to laugh after only one joke, especially in a situation
where they're not expecting humor. They may not believe
their ears after the first one, but after two or three they'll
usually catch on and start to have fun. Sometimes the
speaker or comic tries line after line, and the audience is
totally unmoved. But when just one joke breaks through,
then everyone suddenly perks up, perhaps thinking,
"That was pretty funny. Maybe he's not so bad after all."
They become more receptive, the speaker gets more confident, and an unhappy experience is avoided by both.

How Big Is the Audience?

It's important to be aware of the size of your audience. In a small group the laughter should come quickly—but a *very* small group can present problems. If you're in close quarters—for example, sitting around a table in a conference room—it's best to keep humor brief and as informal as possible. That means that personalized one-liners, rather than story jokes, will probably be best appreciated. When just a few people are gathered, they tend to be too self-conscious to laugh. Laughter *is* contagious—that's why they have laugh tracks on TV sitcoms—and it's very slow to spread if there aren't enough "carriers"! One way to offset this is to try and make sure that people are seated close together, if possible. See if you can have extra chairs removed from a large room. People laugh easier when the person next to them is laughing—as long as that person isn't in the next zip code.

If you do find yourself facing a small, spread-out crowd, don't panic when you don't hear or see any demonstrative response to your jokes. Although they'll hesitate to laugh out loud, this doesn't mean they won't be able to enjoy your remarks as much as they would in a full house. When I started out as a comic, and often performed for late-night audiences of seven or eight people, I would leave the stage totally shaken and discouraged by the deafening silence I encountered. I was always sure that they *hated* me, because not one of their little band would make a sound during my act.

Yet without fail, one or two—or several—would approach me afterward to tell me how much they enjoyed my performance! A club owner finally explained it to me: "They sat quiet because they were *listening* to you. You can't expect to hear laughs like when there are 50 people out there. If they didn't like you, they would've been talking among themselves!" So sometimes, even when you're going for laughs, silence is golden.

There are an infinite number of variables affecting the reaction of any size group, and an infinite number of reasons why, on a given day or night, they might not laugh at your funniest remarks. If you're the first speaker of a morning program, for example, expect a subdued crowd. Even if they seem awake and alert, people are simply not conditioned to start laughing early in the day. Perhaps they need to settle in to reality first, and experience some of their normal routine, before they're willing or able to accept the slightly twisted perceptions of a humorous outlook. The last speaker of the evening or afternoon should not generally expect too great a response either, for obvious reasons—the audience is often too worn out to react demonstratively, even if they do enjoy your presentation.

So if you don't always hear the laughter you feel you deserve, try not to take it personally. It has happened— and will continue to happen—even to the top pros. It's a kind of an occupational hazard for the speaker who dares to try and lighten up his presentation and actually entertain his audience a bit. Besides, such experiences build character—I think.

If you're fortunate enough to be speaking before a very large group in a very big room, you'll find that the laughter will seem to come in three "waves," and it's imperative to adjust the timing of your delivery. First, the people sitting right in front will respond, along with a scattered few who were quickest to get the joke. A fraction of a second later, the majority of the rest of the audience will follow. Finally you'll get the remainder of them—people who took longer to get the joke and those who are only laughing because everyone else is. Bill Rafferty, former cohost of TV's "Real People" and a fine comic as well, summed it up with this simple tip: "When you're performing in a large space, always play to the *back* of the room. They're the people who are hardest to reach." It follows logically, then, that when using humor, you'll take longer to deliver a speech to a large crowd—so be sure to allow for this when you time your presentation.

Speaking of people who are hard to reach, let me say a word about outdoor audiences: Ugh! Outdoor crowds, large or small, are by far the hardest to work with when you're using humor. Too many distractions, compounded by typically poor sound systems, make it very hard (although not impossible) to deliver humor effectively. In that type of situation you simply have to intensify your delivery and hope for the best. Don't merely punch the joke out, *hammer* it over. Try to consciously be more forceful, more animated, and more confident. And it wouldn't hurt to cut down on the amount of humor you would normally use.

Don't Give Yourself Away: Surprise Them

I mentioned earlier how a business speaker has the advantage of lower audience expectations when using humor. One sure way to destroy this advantage is to announce to your audience that you're about to tell a joke. We've all heard people plod into a joke with, "That reminds me of a funny story . . . " or "Yesterday I heard a funny story that I'd like to pass on to you . . . " Speakers who do this are setting themselves up for a fall. It takes away the element of surprise and raises expectations—to the *danger* level. Don't tell your audience you're going to try and make them laugh—just do it! The idea is to get into it before the audience realizes it's a joke. Slip into your setup as casually as you can. One way to succeed at this is to make it seem real: remember to *personalize* and *localize* as we discussed in Chapter 2. One of those simple, personalized lead-ins like "Bill Smith was telling me about . . . " is all you need to get smoothly into a joke.

Getting back into the serious part of the speech *after* the joke also creates problems for some speakers. Don't say, "To get back to the point . . . " or the hackneyed "But seriously . . . " Don't say anything. Change your inflection, your rate of delivery, your tone of voice, or your facial expression—any subtle physical change you feel comfortable with. That's really all it takes to alert the audience that you're getting back to business.

Act Spontaneous, Even If You're Not

The best way to deliver a joke in a speech (or anytime) is to *make it appear spontaneous.* People always show a greater appreciation for humor that seems to come out of the moment. It's particularly helpful when faced with a "cold" audience. The key to loosening up an unresponsive group is to gain their respect, and a sharp ad-lib can often do it best.

I'd like to give you step-by-step guidelines on how to ad-lib successfully on any occasion. I'd like to, but unfortunately, it's impossible. The only people guaranteed to be good ad-libbers are those who are born naturally witty. This probably eliminates 99 percent of us. It's kind of like what you often hear football and basketball coaches say: "You can teach the fundamentals, but you can't teach quickness." The ability to ad-lib, like athletic ability, is something you either have or you don't. But also like athletic ability, people have it in different degrees, and it can be developed—to a point—if you work at it.

How to Be a Wit in Three Easy (?) Lessons

The keys to improving your ad-lib ability are (as you might have guessed) deceptively simple:

Keep a clear head.   In other words, don't panic. Look on an interruption as an opportunity to shine. The moment an interruption occurs, start thinking about how to turn it to your advantage. How? Basically, just . . .

Face the truth of the situation.   As with any kind of humor, an acknowledgment of the simple truth is often the funniest thing you can say. For example, I watched one speaker really get angry at the podium (partly for effect). A beefy guy who was known by his audience to be expressive and excitable, he waved his arms and got red in the face at one point—and proceeded to bump the microphone and send it crashing loudly to the floor. As he picked it up, he said in a subdued tone, "You should see me when I really get mad."

Don't pass up any opportunities to try 'em out.   This means you have to take risks. Whenever something happens that cries out for an ad-lib, take a shot at it— even if you're not sure you should. It doesn't have to be perfect. Ad-libs will get laughs a lot easier than prepared jokes, simply because of the situation: the audience appreciates your effort in a tough spot. If you take some chances, you'll be surprised at how often you'll come out looking good. Your confidence will build, you'll take even more chances, and eventually you may turn out to be a pretty fair ad-libber.

Sometimes You Have to Fake It

I'll be the first to admit that all this sounds easier than it is. As I said at the beginning, it takes a natural-born wit to be a truly great ad-libber. But while one can't really learn to be spontaneous, learning the next best thing—how to appear spontaneous—is not very hard. And it works just as well as the real thing.

The very first time I performed comedy in a club provides a good example of this. My knees were shaking, my material was marginal, and the crowd was silent. Things went from bad to horrible when a sloppy drunk began to heckle me. Well, he wasn't so much heckling me directly—that would have meant he was acknowledging my existence—as he was repeating things I said and mulling them over very loudly to himself. As I contemplating wrapping the microphone cord around my neck and ending it all right there, I remembered the single "heckler response line" I had memorized for just such an unlikely situation as this. I stopped mumbling my jokes and shouted out, "Look, I've only five minutes here to make an ass of myself . . . you've got the rest of your life!"

The crowd burst into laughter and applause, further helping me to silence the loudmouth. Suddenly they were on my side. I did a little more of my act and finally got a few laughs (on jokes that were not all that strong), and left the stage feeling that I would not kill myself after all— I owed that much to my "fans." My seemingly ad-libbed remark had saved the day.

Practice, Practice, Practice

Hopefully, you will never be faced with that kind of situation. But even if you're not, it will obviously be to your great advantage to make all your humorous comments sound as spontaneous as possible. And the way to do this is through careful preparation. Only when you have your material down cold will you be comfortable enough with it to relax and appear as if you're ad-libbing.

Practice each joke aloud, paying attention to pacing, timing, and vocal inflection, until you can recall it without effort. If you can do that, you should be enough at ease to create the illusion of spontaneity. If you're busy trying to remember the punch line as you're delivering the setup to a joke, you're more likely to come off sounding about as glib as a beaten boxer trying to explain his defeat to Howard Cosell.

Watch Your Body Language

Another key to appearing natural when telling a joke is to *be aware of your body language.* Nonverbal communication often gives away a lot of secrets. If you really don't believe in your material, for example, you may involuntarily mumble, or cover your mouth with your hand, or back away from the podium as you deliver a line. And we've all been disturbed by the kind of speaker who stares off into the space above our heads as he talks, or repeatedly pushes his glasses back up the bridge of his nose, or constantly smoothes his hair or scratches his ear (or worse). This is poor form for any kind of speaker; for one trying to be funny, it's deadly. Never forget that when you are on the podium, all eyes are on you. You are the center of attention, and every little gesture or nervous habit is observed by and has its effect on the audience. Let's face it, there are enough psychological barriers between the speaker and his audience—don't allow physical distractions to add to this.

Make eye contact. Just move your focus around the room and pick out individuals. When you deliver the punch line to a joke, deliver it directly to someone. If you're able to catch a person's eye, he or she will feel obliged to laugh—making you feel more confident as you go along.

Convince yourself that you're talking to an individual, not a crowd, and that you like that individual. And vice versa: believe this individual likes you. Your attitude should be this: If I were at a party and met someone like me, would I like them? Would I want to engage them in conversation? Would I enjoy being around them? Say yes or you're reading the wrong book.

Conversely, think of the qualities of people you find the most boring. Generally, they're long-winded; they either try to talk over your head or they're condescending; they often dislike everyone and everything and aren't afraid to say so; they frequently use obscenities. Learn from them how *not* to be.

Don't be afraid to come out from behind the podium if the sound system allows. Remember, the audience likes you better if you're one of them. If you're behind a stand with a removable microphone, you may want to take the mike in your hand and put the stand behind you. Anything you can do to remove barriers is going to be to your advantage. Why do you think comedians (and evangelists) often go right down into the audience to deliver their messages?

When you practice your delivery, do it in front of a mirror, and make sure to devote part of your rehearsal time to body language. Again, being *totally* prepared is the key to a spontaneous style.

Tricks of the Trade

There are several little tricks that professionals use to make a joke seem spontaneous. For example, look for opportunities to make reference to your physical surroundings: the size, decor, or temperature of the room. Comment on a previous speaker, or on his introduction of you. Or perhaps tie your humor in to the day's news.

It can be a simple matter to visit the place you're going to be speaking before you give the speech, or to find out who's scheduled to speak before you on the program, or who's going to introduce you. When you have this kind of information in advance, it's easy to prepare an ad-lib that will convince any audience that you thought of it right on the spot. Of course, if you really are a natural wit, you might be able to pull this off with just some literally last-minute preparation. President Kennedy was known to listen carefully to those speakers who appeared on a program before him and scribble down notes on certain things they said. He would then come up with appropriate humorous remarks and, when it was his turn at the podium, would proceed to charm the audience with his obviously quick wit. Try it—you may surprise yourself. Remember, an ad-lib always impresses listeners more than a "prepared" joke, and does not have to be as funny to get an appreciative reaction.

Making a funny remark on the day's news can also be quite easy. In fact, you don't even have to create a joke that very day; all you have to do is give the appearance that you have. For example, here's a fairly generic joke about the economy:

They say the economy is bouncing back. Unfortunately, so are a lot of our customers' checks.

To make this an up-to-the-minute topical remark, simply preface it with a newspaper headline. The stock market goes up or down every day, doesn't it? Watch:

I saw in the paper today that the stock market was up ten points. I don't know, they say the economy is bouncing back . . . but so are a lot of our customers' checks.

It would work just as well with the opposite news:

I see the market was down another ten points today. I guess the economy is not quite bouncing back . . . but a lot of our customers' checks are.

You'll find many jokes like this. Things that remain topical over a period of years—the economy, ecology, even the weather—can be made to sound as fresh as today's news just through the use of current headlines in the setup. Listen carefully to the "topical" political jokes that Bob Hope uses. Only the names of the politicians are changed from year to year; the jokes are timeless. I'll discuss this in greater detail in the next chapter when covering how to "switch" jokes.

"Ad-libs" to Keep in Mind—Just in Case

Still another way to appear to be a natural wit is to *have comments ready for unusual circumstances.* Anyone who speaks on a regular basis knows that things don't always go just the way we plan. A microphone can go dead, the lights can go out, a podium can topple over— little things like that. Don't ignore obvious distractions. When something interrupts your presentation, it's up to you to put the audience at ease again and regain their attention.

While it's impossible to anticipate and prepare for everything that might happen, it's certainly worth some thought. A comedian friend of mine took a very clever approach. He made a list of everything he could think of that might create a distraction while he was onstage in a nightclub: mikes going dead, glasses breaking, people talking loudly, and even buses roaring down the street outside the club. He then proceeded to sit down and write (or borrow) a "spontaneous" comment for each situation. By preparing this way, he was always able to turn potentially negative situations to his advantage, as he consistently delighted audiences with his ad-libs for all occasions. You can just as easily do the same.

Think about all the things you'd dread to have happen during a presentation. What if the pages of your speech fall to the floor in disarray? What if the slide projector conks out? Or you trip over the wires? And is that room going to pick up street noise, or sounds from the room next door? It's possible to turn any of these distractions into a positive thing—if you're *prepared* to be spontaneous!

To start you off, here are a few situations that might occur and some comments that might be appropriate. And remember, if you're not comfortable with these, that practically *anything* you say will get a laugh when you appear to be ad-libbing.

When you lose your place or pause too long:
I just wanted to wait a moment in case any of you have lost your place.
Sometimes we say the most with silence . . . not this time, but sometimes.
If anyone wants to jump right in here, it's okay with me.
I thought I'd give you a chance to absorb what we've covered so far.

If any of you have heard me speak before . . . please go on to my next thought and I'll catch up.

When you garble a sentence:
Sorry, these are rented lips.
Later on I'll pass out a printed translation of that sentence.
Sorry, it's my first day with a new mouth.
The next time I speak, I'll have subtitles.
By the way, the rest of my speech will be dubbed in English. I invested $1,000 fixing my eyes, Now my mouth doesn't work.

When the microphone goes dead:
Some people say my speeches are better when the mike's not working.
Evidently someone has heard this speech before.
Maybe I'll just pass around the printed text and we'll break up into discussion groups.
Let me have a show of hands . . . how many of you can read lips?
This is what happens when you buy your sound system at Woolworth's.

Microphone feedback:
That concludes the musical portion of the program.
Don't be alarmed . . . this is only a test.

When people are talking during your presentation:
Feel free to talk among yourselves.
Excuse me for talking while you're interrupting.
I try to give my presentation the same way you have a romantic evening . . . alone.
Please—I've only got tonight to make a fool of myself. You've got the rest of your life.

When the lights go out (or flicker):
This is taking energy conservation a bit too far.
Why do I have the feeling that when the lights come back on, I'll be alone?
I told them not to ignore a final bill.
I forgot to mention we have a curfew tonight.
Was it something I said?

When the lights come back on:
Everyone stay where you are—I'm taking another head count.

Loud crashing noise during presentation:
That concludes the musical portion of the program.
(At banquet) I hope that wasn't my dessert.

When the room is too cold:
I tried to get the janitor to turn on some heat . . . but he said he had to go feed the polar bears.
I tried to turn up the thermostat . . . but it had already frozen over.

When the room is too hot:
I tried to get the janitor to lower the heat . . . but I was chased off by some guy with a red suit and a pitchfork.
I tried to lower the thermostat . . . but it was already melted.

If you've absorbed everything up to this point in the book, you probably know all the average speaker needs to know about selecting and delivering appropriate humor in a business presentation. And now you have the necessary background to become your own comedy writer—as you will see in the following chapter.

A CHECKLIST FOR PREPARATION
Occasion (conference, workshop, retirement)
Your position on schedule (early morning, late afternoon)
Other speakers/entertainment
Your introduction
Room size
Acoustics
Microphone or not?
Distance of podium from audience
Possible distractions/interruptions
Any unusual circumstances

CHAPTER 4

Everything Old Is New Again

Switching Jokes to Fit Your Needs

This chapter explains "switching," a technique used by professional comedy writers to transform inadequate jokes into winners and to increase their output of humor in general. The chapter teaches:

➢ The four kinds of switching: how to switch setup, punch line, concept, and time frame
➢ A five-step technique that makes it easy
➢ How to "polish" your jokes to ensure they'll generate the greatest impact in the clearest possible way

> Seven guidelines for polishing that guarantee your
  joke will be worded in a way that minimizes the chance
  for misunderstanding

> > >

Many years ago I used to do a joke that went: "My grand-father is really getting old. Last year his insurance company sent him his free calendar one month at a time." It generally got a polite laugh.

A little later, during Ronald Reagan's 1980 presidential campaign, I changed it to: "Everyone knows Reagan is getting old. Last year his insurance company sent him his free calendar one month at a time." This got a bigger laugh because, although the joke was not really new, the addition of Reagan's name made it "topical."

Still later, when I needed a joke for a corporate speaker talking about a company in the red, it became: "Everyone knows this business is in trouble. Last year our insurance company sent us our free calendar one month at a time." This was eventually refined to "You know your business is in trouble when your insurance company sends you half a calendar."

A business in trouble would seem to have little in common with a person who's getting old, but both were served by essentially the same joke. That's the beauty of switching—the process of changing a joke to update it, topicalize it, slant it to your audience, or simply make it funnier.

The best analogy I can give you to explain switching comes from the New Testament. Ever hear of the miracle of the loaves and fishes? (Those of you more familiar with the Old Testament should recall the story of manna raining from heaven.) Switching also creates much from little. Somewhere you may have heard the theory that there are only seven basic jokes and all others are just variations of those. By the end of this chapter you may agree. We'll first discuss the four basic kinds of switch, and then explain a step-by-step technique for switching. If you get nothing else out of this book, learn this skill, and you will always have access to a fresh supply of jokes.

Switch the Setup

Changing the setup of a joke is the simplest form of switching, but is still very effective in redirecting a humorous remark. For example, here's a joke that can be made appropriate for a retirement roast:

He's such a dumb jock, he won a gold medal in the Olympics and he had it bronzed.

How, you may ask, is this related to retirement? Look at the idea that actually makes the joke funny, what we'll call the *key element:* having a gold object bronzed. If we keep this key element and change the setup to suit our needs, we come up with:

Earlier today we gave him the traditional gold watch. He was so happy that he had it bronzed.

Now that we've identifed the key element, almost any gold object can be substituted to fit the altered setup:

At her retirement dinner, they gave her a gold necklace. . . .

Or a gold bracelet, cigarette case, or lighter. Gold *coins* might inspire a new setup:

When I was a child my grandfather gave me his collection of gold coins. I was so happy, I had them bronzed.

All of these jokes come from the same basic punch line; only the setups have been altered. Now let's look at a slightly more difficult kind of switching.

Switch the Punch Line

Switching the punch line serves a different purpose. Instead of making an irrelevant joke appropriate, as when switching the setup, you start with one already appropriate joke and create more from it. Like this one:

I'm the youngest of our company's corporate officers. It doesn't bother me too much . . . except when people send me memos written in crayon.

The key element here is the idea of an adult executive being treated like a child. Switching the punch line along these lines while keeping the same setup might result in:

I'm the youngest of our company's corporate officers. It doesn't bother me too much . . . except that I can't leave my office without a hall pass.

or

It doesn't bother me too much . . . except that when I'm out sick, I have to bring in a note from my mother.

There are numerous possibilities for more jokes in this mold. There is a more complex kind of switching, however, that can yield an almost limitless variety of material.

Switch the Concept

Switching the concept of a joke is not as straightforward as simply changing the setup or punch line. It requires a little more creative thinking—but it's well worth the effort. Our example starts with an old (but funny) one-liner:

My neighborhood was so tough, when we were kids we didn't play doctor, we played autopsy.

It takes a moment to extract the key element here, but it appears to be the idea of a "different" type of kids game—one with an adult slant. If you think of children's games and give them an adult twist, you get:

I always knew Joan would grow up to be a real estate agent. As a kid she never played house . . . she played condominium.

or

Bill was always ahead of his time. As a kid he never played doctor . . . he played holistic health practitioner.

A variation from simply using games would be to use other things kids do:

It was always obvious Harold would grow up to be an accountant. As a kid he never wanted to read books . . . he just wanted to balance them.

All these jokes are much further removed from the originals than the jokes in the earlier examples, but their essence is the same. One could even go further and use the proper name of a well-known subject:

It was obvious that Conrad Hilton was going to be a success in his profession. As a kid he never played house, he played hotel.

And this takes us full circle, back to a very old joke that is another variation on this theme:

Henry Haverstock

When Rockefeller [or fill in rich family name] was a kid, his father bought him a set of blocks—Fifth Avenue, Park Avenue, 42nd Street, ...

Switch the Time Frame

There is another kind of switching that is really a combination of all the others. By switching the time frame, or historical context, or whatever you want to call it, you can update most topical jokes from different eras. For example, here's a joke from the post—World War II 1940s:

I don't know why they make such a big deal about Washington throwing a dollar across the Potomac. Truman's throwing millions across the Atlantic.

This was a reference to the Marshall Plan, by which U.S. money helped to rebuild Europe after the war. In the 1960s, during the war in Vietnam, this same joke might have worked with just a change of names in the punch line:

. . . LBJ's throwing millions across the Pacific.

In the 1980s it might work as:

. . . Reagan's throwing millions across the Caribbean.

The same joke can be made relevant to widely different eras if the basic idea is sound—simply by updating the names. This kind of switching reinforces a basic belief behind the technique: there is no such thing as an old joke.

A Step-by-Step Technique for Switching

If some of these switches seem to have been accomplished a little too smoothly and much too fast—you're right. I left out the actual mechanics of getting from A to B to C so as not to get in the way of the examples. Anyway, after one has been writing comedy for a long time, it really does work that easily, since it becomes instinctive after doing it enough. But even a novice can learn the basic technique very quickly, simply by taking it one step at a time. And that's what we're going to do right now.

1. *Pick a joke.* In the beginning, the jokes you decide to switch should be those you think are funny. That way, you're spared much of the effort of trying to *make* them funny. As you gain more experience, you'll see that they really don't have to start out funny—after all, one of the advantages of switching is precisely that it gives you the means to rejuvenate seemingly lifeless material. More important than starting out with a funny joke is to start with a clearly *structured* gag that you can understand perfectly. By structured, I mean one that has a straightforward, easy-to-see setup and punch line. Like this:

Beverly Hills is such a rich town, even the mailman carries a Gucci bag.

Simple. Setup ("Beverly Hills is such a rich town . . .), pause (comma), punch line (" . . . even the mailman carries a Gucci bag").

2. Identify the key element of the joke. What makes it funny? What is the joke saying that distorts reality just a bit, while still keeping close to the truth? If we analyze the mailman joke along these lines, the "generic" joke idea seems to be that the *mailman* in a *rich place* carries a *designer bag.* Once you identify where the laugh is coming from, you can start using your imagination.

3. Break down the key element into its separate components and extend them. At this stage, just a few word associations are all you need. Think about the broader categories represented by "mailman," "rich place," and "designer bag." In general, if the component is specific, extend it to the general. If it's general, extend it to the specific. In the case of "mailman," a specific job, we would list *occupations* and *government agencies.* For "rich places" we might think of wealthy *cities, countries,* and *streets,* or places like expensive *stores, hotels,* and *restaurants.* "Designer bag" can be extended to simply *expensive things.*

4. List associations for each component. This is where you can let your imagination run wild. Make a list for all of the extended components. I'll start you off with some short lists, but don't limit or edit yourself at this point.

Cities, Countries, Streets	*Stores, Hotels, Restaurants*
Palm Springs	Nieman-Marcus
Park Avenue	The Plaza Hotel
Saudi Arabia	Chasen's
Rodeo Drive	The Polo Lounge

You can probably see how easy it would be to switch the setup of the original joke to whatever locale was appropriate:

Palm Springs is such a rich town, even the mailman carries a Gucci bag.

And so forth. But that's too easy. Let's go a little further and experiment with the punch line. Our association lists might look like this:

Occupations	Government Agencies	Expensive Things
paper boy	Social Security	Rolls Royce
doctor	Defense	valet parking
store clerk	Department	yacht
construction	motor vehicles	anything gold
	unemployment	

Write down anything that comes to mind along these lines. Items on a list may suggest whole new categories. For example:

Government agencies
Defense Department
Navy
Weapons
Battleships
Store clerk
Grocery stores
Expensive foods
Inflation

When you've extended each list and each item as far as you possibly can, you're ready for the final step.

5. *Create rough jokes.* This is the fun part. By selective mixing and matching from your lists—keeping in mind

the basic premise of the original joke—and throwing in a little more imagination, you can plug in a variety of new jokes, with straightforward switches of setup and punch line:

In a supermarket on Rodeo Drive, the clerk packed my groceries in a Gucci bag.

In Saudi Arabia they're so rich, the paper boy drives a Rolls Royce.

The doctors on Park Avenue use gold-plated tongue depressors.

The Palm Springs unemployment office has valet parking.

These are not perfect jokes—yet. It's again important not to start editing yourself at this stage. Just write down any idea that strikes you as having funny possibilities—anything with potential. Later on you can concentrate on polishing these diamonds in the rough (we'll learn how in the next part of this chapter). The main objective now is to get rough joke ideas on paper.

While you're at it, try to keep in mind the four kinds of switching we mentioned at the beginning of the chapter. The jokes I've created in this example so far have illustrated simple switches in the setup and the punch line—but what about switching the essence, or concept of the joke? Let's go back to our extended list of associations for *government agencies*:

Government agencies
Defense Department
Navy

Weapons
Battleship

This kind of free-form association is the key to switching the concept. Remember, we started with "mailman," and now we've gotten to "battleship"—quite a jump! It takes some familiarity with switching before this becomes easy, but it usually works well. With a little thought, you might come up with these:

I think the navy is spending too much money . . . they just bought another battle-yacht.

I think the army is spending too much money . . . they're now issuing Gucci duffel bags.

As you can see, we've come a long way from that first joke—and created a whole array of new material.

Switch a Story to Make a New Point

Although all of our examples so far have been one-liners, switching is by no means limited to that kind of joke. Longer stories can be switched just as effectively, but you are a little more limited in what you can do. There are usually so many converging elements in a good story that it's necessary to retain most of them or the joke loses its impact. In many cases, however, you can switch the punch line and change the point of the joke without hurting the laugh.

Let's go back to our beloved airplane joke. In the original version, the bad news is "We're totally lost." The good news is "We're way ahead of schedule." Suppose you wanted to use an adaptation of this joke when talking about the overabundance of restrictive government regulations. You might change the good news to "You don't have to go through customs" to make a point, as one client of mine did.

Another approach to changing this story might be to reverse the order of the good news and bad news, and work from there. For example, "First the good news— we're way ahead of schedule. The bad news is . . . " If your point is, say, the conservation (or waste) of resources, the bad news might be "We're out of gas."

Polish Your Rough Jokes into Finished Gems

Polishing is the process that turns a funny concept into a joke, or makes a joke funnier and easier to understand. It can also help you avoid "telegraphing" the punch line (giving it away too soon), and helps enhance the element of surprise that is so important in humor. Most of the standard rules of good writing apply as well to joke writing; in fact, they should be practiced even more fervently. Writing jokes is actually a lot like writing poetry: you're striving for the maximum impact with the minimum of words. And like poetry, jokes are meant to be spoken aloud, so they should also have a sense of rhythm. Here are some guidelines for polishing:

1. Use your speaking—not writing—vocabulary. When polishing jokes, you must always be aware of the difference between the written and spoken word. Since your jokes are meant to be said aloud, use everyday, conversational language. Choose words that are easy to understand and easy to say: "a lot," not "an abundance of," or "said," not "asserted." The idea is to use words and sentence structures that allow the audience to grasp the point right away, without delay or confusion. As we mentioned in Chapter 3, always read the joke aloud. It should roll smoothly off the tongue. If there are words or phrases you stumble over, take them out! Examine each word in the joke and ask yourself if you can take it out and still make the joke work. There should be absolutely no extra words (I was about to say "excess verbiage"). Remember Henny Youngman's classic tribute to brevity in humor: "Take my wife . . . please!"

2. *Eliminate structural faults.* The common grammatical flaws you learned about in English 101 are even more damaging in jokes. For example, *don't avoid the subject.* This often occurs in sentences that begin with "it" or "there," such as "There's a bonus given by the boss . . . " instead of the more succinct "The boss gives a bonus . . . " As you learned in basic English class, a sentence should generally be structured subject–verb–object.

It's also important to *use active verbs.* Referring again to the example above, the first phrase is passive: "There's a bonus given. . . ." The second version says it more actively: " . . . gives a bonus. . . . " So don't say, "George Lucas has a new movie out"; say, "George Lucas released a new movie." Avoid *all* passive constructions like "has been," "seems to have," "was going," and the like.

Always try to be as succinct as possible with your verb structures. Sloppy joke writers often overuse the infinitive "to be," as in "Inflation seems to be getting out of control." Just say, "Inflation is out of control," or better yet, choose more vivid words and say "Inflation is skyrocketing," or "going through the roof"—get the picture? Good—that's exactly the idea.

Along with subjects and verbs, adjectives are another misused part of speech that can hurt your jokes. Be sure to *use direct modifiers.* Don't say, "A salesman who showed signs of nervousness," but rather "a nervous salesman." Always try to keep the adjective close to the word it modifies.

3. *Use the right word.* We've already talked at length about the importance of personalizing and localizing. Those are two aspects of using the right word. The right word is very often the more specific word: I used *Lemon Pledge*, not "a furniture polish." I had a piña colada, not "a drink." I was a stunt man for *Masters and Johnson*, not "a sex clinic." My parents left me on a doorstep of a moving *Winnebago*, not "a motor home." Place names, brand names, and the like always give the audience a clearer mental image and help you create the verbal cartoon that a good joke should be.

The Marx Brothers once made a movie called *The Cocoanuts* (1929). Somehow I don't think it would have been as funny a picture if they had called it *The Tropical Fruit*. "Cocoanuts" is one of those inherently funny words. It's funny for the same reasons "prunes" are funnier than "grapes," or "cantaloupes" are funnier than "apples." There's a wonderful scene in Neil Simon's play/movie *The Sunshine Boys* where an old vaudeville comic rants and raves to his young nephew: "Words with a *K* are funny! Words with a *C* are funny! Words with a *Z* are funny!" He's right. Why is "cockroach" funnier than "ant"? I'm not really sure. This is clearly an area where your comic instincts must come into play.

4. *Remember the rule of three.* At some time over the last 25 years, you've probably heard Johnny Carson follow a joke that died with an aside like, "I should have remembered: Never do more than three on a subject." Carson often refers to comedy's Rule of Three because—well, it's not to be trifled with. But it goes beyond not doing more

than three jokes per topic. Think for a moment about how many jokes begin with "There was a priest, a minister, and a rabbi" or "a Frenchman, an Englishman, and an Italian." Think of the narratives in other jokes, both long and short, that involve a series of three actions or a list of three items, with the punch line coming on the third. You know what I mean:

Trick or treating in Beverly Hills can be very lucrative. Last year my kid got six apples, four candy bars, and two points in the next Spielberg picture.

I believe this has to do in part with the poetic aspect of jokes that I mentioned earlier. Rhythm is often built in (probably unconsciously) to the best jokes. If you listen to a "rapid-fire" comic like Henny Youngman or Rodney Dangerfield, you'll find that their use of rhythm (combined with excellent timing) sets you up to laugh at regular intervals—sort of "on the beat"—and sometimes you're laughing whether the joke's there or not, simply because you're caught up in that rhythm!

5. *Show—don't tell—what was said.* Ever notice how, when you're reading a book, you tend to gobble up passages of dialogue, but slow down a bit through the narrative parts? Most people prefer to be shown things rather than told them. It's the same in jokes: always try to reduce narrative and increase quotes. Look at the two versions of this example:

Wrong:

My kid is not doing too well in school. His teacher asked him who Betsy Ross was, and he said he thought she used to be the lead singer in the Supremes.

Right:

My kid is not doing too well in school. His teacher asked him, "Who was Betsy Ross?" and he said, "I think she used to be the lead singer in the Supremes."

An individual quote should never be divided in a joke. Printed versions of jokes often feature divided quotes like: "It's possible," said the farmer, "but you'll have to share a room." This may look okay in written form, but it makes a smooth verbal delivery more difficult. Keep quotes continuous, as: The farmer said, "It's possible, but you'll have to share a room."

6. *Make sure the punch line is at the end.* We've already discussed this in Chapter 3, but it just can't be emphasized too much, especially when polishing. Sometimes a joke that seems funny but just won't work is simply suffering from a misplaced punch line. It's not always discernible right away. Study each joke carefully to determine exactly where the laugh is supposed to come from, and then put that word or phrase as close to the end as possible, with no extra words after it. Here's another example (using a standard joke that was switched to become topical during the summer of 1981):

Wrong:

During the baseball strike, Howard Cosell will be lifting weights with his tongue to stay in shape.

Right:

During the baseball strike, Howard Cosell intends to stay in shape by lifting weights . . . with his tongue.

Note that nothing follows the key word. And up until "tongue" occurs, the listener has no idea of where this is leading—which maximizes the element of surprise, and in turn, the laugh response.

7. Reveal enough, but not too much information: the ah-ha principle. Closely tied to the element of surprise, but still an entity unto itself, is what is known in comedy as the Ah-ha Principle. "Ah-ha" refers to that moment when the listener "gets" the joke. He makes a new connection between things, or sees them in a different relationship, not because you have pointed it out, but because you have led him to a point where he can figure it out himself. The Ah-ha Principle is the key to most of the best jokes because it lets the audience fill in the blank, that is, you provide point A and C, and they fill in connecting point B. Here's an example:

I think my wife is fooling around. Our dog keeps bringing my slippers to the mailman.

Did you pause for a fraction of a second after "mailman" and make a comic discovery? (I hope so, it's my joke.) Notice how you were provided with two bits of information and then invited to fill in the rest yourself:

Wife is fooling around: C (end result)
Dog brings slippers to mailman: A (evidence)
The connection of the two above: B (Ah-ha!)

Here's another one from Tom Finnigan:

My sister used to be a teller in a sperm bank. One day she came to work pregnant, and they arrested her for embezzlement.

The ah-ha here occurs when the listener gets to complete the analogy: *embezzlement* is to *bank* as *pregnant* is to *sperm bank*. After "embezzlement" the mind races back through the joke to the setup and—ah-ha—a connection!

There are no rules or techniques for employing the Ah-ha Principle (oh, that there only were). All you can do is be constantly aware of it when writing or switching, and let your natural sense of humor guide you.

If you've mastered the art of switching jokes and polishing jokes, you'll find no difficulty in creating your own, original jokes—as you'll learn to do in the next chapter.

A SWITCHING CHECKLIST
1. Pick a joke.

2. Identify the key element in the joke.

3. Break down the key element into its separate components and extend them.

4. List associations for each component.

5. Create rough jokes.

A POLISHING CHECKLIST
1. Use your speaking—not writing—vocabulary.

2. Eliminate structural faults.

3. Use the right word.

4. Remember the Rule of Three.

5. Show—don't tell—what was said.

6. Make sure the punch line is at the end.

7. Reveal enough, but not too much information: the Ah-ha Principle.

CHAPTER 5

Not Quite Technical Writing

Creating Your Own Humor

This chapter details:

➤ Six joke-writing formulas used by professional comedy writers: exaggeration, reverse, substitution, cliché, combination, and definition
➤ Step-by-step instructions for creating each type of joke
➤ Numerous examples of each category

➤   ➤   ➤

When I tell people I write jokes, one of the first questions they always ask me is, "How do you think of 'em?" Most people seem to believe that creating humor is some mystical process of divine inspiration that only a gifted few are capable of. The reality, however, is that (1) joke writing is a learnable skill that anyone with a sense of humor can master, and (2) if you wait for inspiration, you're not going to get very much on paper.

Professional comedy writers don't wait for inspiration—they usually don't have the time. They approach their writing as a craft, not necessarily an art (artists tend to starve; you never hear of a "starving craftsman"). To me, writing jokes is very much like any other desk job in that you must sit down and grind out the work in a given time period. I will admit, though, it's more fun to grind out jokes than actuarial tables! The point is, a comedy writer cannot afford the luxury of writer's block. And most pros are generally able to avoid it because, when they are writing, they are always aware (consciously or not) of the basic joke structures—formulas, if you will—that give them a constant framework within which to work.

Don't misunderstand. Writing humor is a marvelously creative, stimulating process. But like everything else in life, if you break it down you find a great deal of structure and subdivision. The real beauty of joke writing is that there will always be an infinite number of possible jokes that can be drawn from a finite number of joke structures. The top comedy writers prove this point much better than I can. People like Woody Allen and Neil Simon, who are generally accepted by their peers as the finest comedy writers of the past 30-odd years, have always followed the classic joke structures in their work. Of course, not everyone can put brilliant twists on old formulas like these comic geniuses do—but if it's good enough for them, it's sure worth a try for us!

In this chapter we're going to present an overview of the step-by-step techniques for several of the most popular formulas. We're not going to go too deeply into them—just enough to make you aware of them and give you the basics of how to use them. As you'll see from the examples in each section, practically every joke you've ever heard will fall into one of these categories, if not several of them.

It's important to realize from the start that there's going to be some degree of overlap between joke classifications. Some jokes can fit into more than one category. This is not at all important. Learning to categorize jokes is not the object of this chapter; learning to write them is. The formulas are provided so that you have as many tools as possible when you sit down to create humor. So don't get hung up on the different groupings. Concentrate on developing the ability to use all these tricks of the trade to maximize the quantity of the jokes you write. In comedy writing, quantity eventually equals quality, because the more you write, the better you get at it.

Exaggeration Jokes: It Was So Cold That . . .

An exaggeration joke is one in which a quality of a person, place, or thing is stretched to the point of absurdity. You often hear them set up with phrases like "It was so cold that . . ." or "She's so fat that . . ." or (fill in the blanks) " —— is so —— that . . ." Woody Allen wrote my favorite exaggeration joke ever: "I had a very deep cavity. I went to my dentist, and he sent me to a chiropodist." Now, *that's* deep! I also like an old one of Rodney Dangerfield's "The plumbing in my apartment is so bad, if I want to take a bath on Saturday, I have to start the water running on Wednesday." I once wrote one about the venerable old San Francisco attorney Melvin Belli that went: "He's been practicing law for many, many years. In his first case, he defended the victim of a hit-and-run stage-coach. See what's meant by exaggeration? There are a few simple steps to creating an exaggeration joke:

1. Pick a subject. Let's start with *car.*

2. Make a word association list. Using only nouns, list all the associations you can make with *car:* engine, speedometer, headlights, chrome, license plate, glove compartment, shock absorbers, mechanic, and so on.

3. Pick an adjective to describe the subject. I used old to describe Melvin Belli when I used this formula. Let's use this adjective again.

4. Make another word association list. Again use only nouns, but this time those associated with *old:* bifocals, wrinkles, Geritol, truss, liver spots, Medicare, and so on.

These are all associated with old people—but there's no reason to limit yourself to that. What about: dinosaurs, Roman numerals, Dead Sea scrolls, antiques, Stone Age, Old West, and so on. Any period of past history can (and should) be associated with *old.*

5. Connect words on the two lists and then justify the connection. And then you've got a rough joke. For example, connect "speedometer" from the *car* list with "Roman numerals" from the *old* list, and justify it by saying:

That car is so old, the speedometer is in Roman numerals.

Similarly, you might connect "license plates" with "Stone Age" to come up with: That car is so old, the license plate is carved in stone.

Here are a few more rough joke associations. Try expanding on the lists and adding a few of your own:

That car is so old, the engine runs on Geritol.

. . . it's got bifocal headlights.

. . . it goes to a mechanic who takes Medicare.

. . . there are liver spots on the chrome.

. . . instead of shock absorbers, it wears a truss.

. . . there were dinosaur eggs in the glove compartment.

Granted, these are not all terrific jokes, but the formula creates volume and it gets you thinking. The critical part of this process is writing the association lists. It is vital to let your imagination run wild, and write down as many different things as you can possibly connect to your subject or adjective. The more creative you are in making the list, the funnier your jokes will turn out.

Reverse Jokes: Turn It Around

A reverse joke is one in which you turn around a normal sequence of events, words, or mental connections. At the beginning of this chapter I told you that writing jokes merely required that you be able to see the less obvious relationships between things. Reverse jokes are a perfect example of this. Perhaps that's why they're my favorite type of joke. I think of reverses as hard-working, blue-collar jokes—they always give you an honest day's work!

There are two kinds: reverse action and reverse association. Each is created through a similar three-step process. The reverse action joke works like this:

1. Find two actions that normally follow one another. Such as: boiling an egg for three minutes, and then eating it.

2. Turn the order around. This gives us the idea: eating an egg and then boiling it for three minutes. The now-second action will be the punch line of the joke to come.

3. Create a setup to explain the new order. Ask yourself why the actions might now be in this order. In this case, it might be:

He can't cook at all. For breakfast he swallows an egg and then drinks boiling water for three minutes.

Sometimes there's more than one way to reverse an action. Suppose you're starting with: see a peeping tom, pull down the shade. You could reverse it to: pull down the shade, see a peeping tom. Or you might try: see a peeping tom, he pulls down the shade. Then your setup becomes:

I'm so ugly, when a peeping tom saw me he pulled down the shade.

One excellent reverse action joke is Woody Allen's line, "My grandfather was a very insignificant man. At his funeral, the hearse followed the other cars."

The reverse *association* joke is very much the same type of thing:

1. Find two things typically associated in a particular manner. For example, we've all heard of toys with "batteries not included."

2. Turn around the association. Then we have "batteries—toys not included." It's already a perfect punch line.

3. Create a setup to explain the new association. Rodney Dangerfield did it:

When I was a kid, we were so poor I got batteries—toys not included.

Let's try the association, "lined up to get in" to a movie. The reverse would be "lined up to get out." Obviously, "That movie was so bad, they were lined up to get out."

As you can see, reverse jokes are inherently suited to putdowns, so it's no surprise that Rodney Dangerfield has loads of them:

I was such an ugly kid, my mother got morning sickness after I was born.

I was so poor that when my rich aunt died, in the will I owed her twenty dollars.

My wife is a bad cook. In our house we pray after we eat.

Substitution Jokes: Chauffeur-Driven Skateboards and Other Creations

A substitution joke is one which replaces either (1) a concept or (2) a quality of an item with a concept or quality from a different item. The most common of these often use a popular brand name or well-known phrase as a starting point. Substituting for the concept generally requires just three steps:

1. Pick a concept. "Industrial strength cleanser" is a widely known item.

2. Replace a word to change the concept. The new word should be related to the object of your joke. I was writing for a roast when I came up with "industrial strength mouthwash."

3. Create a new setup to explain the substitution. The roast line was: "Sometimes his breath is so bad, he needs industrial strength mouthwash."

You may recall that we used a substitution joke in the previous chapter's switching exercise: ". . . the Army is issuing Gucci duffel bags." Some other examples:

Chauffeur-driven limo:
That kid is so rich, he rides a chauffeur-driven skateboard.

Steel-belted tires:
Arnold Schwarzenegger is so well built, he has to wear a steel-belted undershirt.

Hamburger helper:
The cannibals are trying to stretch their meal budget—they're using Missionary Helper.

Wash-and-wear anything:
She's been married so many times, she owns a wash-and-wear wedding gown.

Substituting a quality involves a slightly more complex technique:

1. Pick a subject. Let's use a toaster.

2. Find one of its obvious qualities. Among other things, we could say it's mechanical.

3. Pick another subject with the same (or somewhat the same) quality. Cars, for instance, are also mechanical.

4. Pick a second quality of the first subject. Toasters also make things pop out.

5. Add this second quality to the second subject. Then you'd have a car that makes things pop out.

6. Justify step 5. I came up with: "I fixed my car with parts from my toaster. Now if I don't wear a seatbelt, I pop out every three minutes."

Sometimes substituting a quality can be a simple, straightforward process. As you gain more experience creating jokes, you'll become more adept at zipping through the steps instinctively. For example, I don't think Woody Allen went through the six steps to substitute a quality of insurance companies in this one:

My wife has orgasmic insurance. If I fail to satisfy her sexually, Mutual of Omaha has to pay her.

Jokes that substitute a quality often overlap with combination jokes, another category we'll get into shortly.

Cliché Jokes: As the Saying Goes

A cliché joke is one that is based on a familiar phrase, proverb, buzzword, title, or the like. Actually, most cliché jokes are either reverse or substitution jokes that happen to use clichés. Take a look at the most common (and, in my opinion, most effective) type, the reverse cliché:

1. Pick a cliché. Such as, "to place someone on a pedestal."

2. Reverse the cliché. Then you would place someone under a pedestal.

3. Explain the reverse. As Woody Allen said, "I had a bad attitude in my marriage. I tended to place my wife under a pedestal."

A second type of cliché joke keeps the order the same, but changes, or substitutes, a word or phrase in it:

1. Pick a cliché. For example, "sitting up with a sick friend."

2. Change a word. "Sitting up with a sick economy."

3. Explain the change. "The president had a rough night. He spent it sitting up with a sick economy."

You can also keep a cliché intact and simply use it as the punch line or the setup—if, as usual, you can explain or justify it. For example, as a setup:

I never forget a face . . . but in your case I'll try.

Or, use a cliché as a punch line, and create a setup to make it funny:

I saw a weird sign in a crematorium—Thank You for Not Smoking.

Combination Jokes: Cross a Mink with a Gorilla

A combination joke is one that takes characteristics from two different items and blends them together in a funny way. Sound familiar? It should—combination jokes often overlap with a lot of other types. In fact, it's sometimes hard to distinguish them from substitution jokes. But as I've said, it's really not important. The only significant difference you need to know about combination jokes is the formula used to create them:

1. *Pick two subjects.* They can be peripherally related or totally unrelated. We'll use "alphabet soup" and "a cup of flour."

2. *List characteristics associated with each subject.*

Alphabet Soup	Cup of Flour
warms stomach	make a cake with it
can spell with letters	people borrow it
comes in a can	white and powdery
eat it with a spoon	make pancakes with it

3. *Connect a characteristic from one list with a characteristic from the other list.* Try "can spell with letters" and "can make pancakes."

4. *Write a rough joke.* I came up with:

The company cafeteria added flour to yesterday's alphabet soup. Today they're serving monogrammed pancakes.

Another form of combination joke is the widely known "What do you get when you cross . . . ?" joke, like:

What do you get when you cross a mink and a gorilla? A mink coat . . . but the sleeves are always too long.

Many "conceptual" routines are made up of combination jokes. Steve Martin's classic bit about his cat embezzling from him is a good example, simply combining the char-

acteristics of a typical cat with those of a typical embez-
zler! Woody Allen once combined his neurotic comic persona with softball to come up with:

I used to play for the neurotic softball team. I would steal
second base, then feel guilty and go back.

Definition Jokes

A definition joke simply defines a word in a comical way.
It's similar to an exaggeration joke in that it magnifies
an aspect of the subject to make it funny. The humor
comes from the fact that the characteristic used to define
the word is generally one that is thought to be of lesser
importance. Here's how to do it:

1. Pick a subject to be defined. How about "Christmas"?

2. List traits associated with the subject. Don't forget
to use negative as well as positive traits: Santa Claus,
Christmas trees, receiving gifts, returning gifts, crowded
stores, singing carols, kissing under the mistletoe. . . .

*3. Pick a trait that isn't commonly used to define the
subject.* Generally, a negative trait will be funnier, as:

Christmas is the time of year when you receive a lot of
presents you can't wait to return.

Definition jokes are used in public speaking a lot more
often than you might realize. I frequently write a "definition" of the place I or a client is going to speak, to be used
as an opening line. For example:

It's great to be in New York City—gateway to New Jersey.

Another popular form of definition joke is the kind I've heard Bob Hope use:

The doctor told me I had a virus. A virus! That's a Latin word meaning, "Your guess is as good as mine."

Use the Formulas Plus Your Natural Sense of Humor

There you have them. As I said at the beginning of the chapter and tried to stress throughout, don't get hung up on the distinctions between the different categories. They're presented this way simply to help you organize and structure your sense of humor so that you can maximize your creative efficiency. They're especially helpful when you think you're "blocked," but they're also good to start on and take off from—if you let your imagination take over after the formulas help you get your juices flowing.

You now know all the basics of selecting, delivering, and creating your own humor. The rest of this book, Part 2, is a source of jokes you can use—and if I do say so myself, it's probably the funniest and most practical source that's available to business speakers. Enjoy!

A CHECKLIST OF JOKE CATEGORIES
Exaggeration
Reverse
Substitution
Cliché
Combination
Definition

The Jokes

CHAPTER 6

One-Liners

Advertising

➤ Advertising brings quick results. Yesterday we advertised for a security guard and last night we were robbed.

➤ Stopping advertising to save money is like stopping your watch to save time.

➤ Advertising is a picture of a beautiful person eating, holding, driving, wearing, or standing in front of something nobody really needs but somebody wants to sell.

➤ Doing business without advertising is like winking at a stranger in the dark. You know what you're doing, but nobody else does.

➤ Advertising is what makes you think you've longed all your life for something that you've never even heard of.

➤ The Golden Rule of public relations is "Do unto others as you would have the six o'clock news do unto you."

➤ Advertising [or public relations] without research is like shooting an arrow into the air and then looking for a target to catch it with.

➤ "Many a small thing has been made large by the right kind of advertising." (Mark Twain)

Age

➤ Old? At his last birthday party the candles cost more than the cake.

➤ There are three signs of old age. The first is loss of memory . . . the other two I forget.

➤ You know you're getting old when people call you young-looking instead of young.

➤ You know you're getting old when your insurance agent sends you his free calendar one month at a time.

➤ Maybe it's true that life begins at forty . . . but everything else starts to wear out.

➤ Middle age is when work is a lot less fun and fun is a lot more work.

➤ Middle age is when it takes longer to rest than to get tired.

➤ Middle age is that time of life when you spend more time talking to your pharmacist than you do to your bartender.

➤ Middle age is when you're sitting at home on a Saturday night, and the phone rings . . . and you hope it isn't for you.

➤ Middle age is when, if you have a choice between two temptations, you choose the one that'll get you home earlier.

➤ "Old men are dangerous: it doesn't matter to them what is going to happen to the world." (George Bernard Shaw)

➤ "I'll never retire because there isn't a thing I can't do now that I didn't do at 18 . . . which gives you an idea of how pathetic I was at 18." (George Burns)

Airlines/Airports

➤ I flew with a very small airline. You had to have exact change to get on the plane.

➤ I flew in on a real discount airline. Instead of a movie, the pilot passed around snapshots of his wife and kids. Or: There was no movie, but they flew very low over drive-in theaters.

➤ The plane made me nervous. The oxygen masks were coin operated . . . and I didn't have exact change.

➤ The airline of course lost my luggage. I'm
used to that, but this time I was a little suspicious—the guy at the baggage claim was wearing
my clothes.

➤ Every year it costs less to fly and more to park
at the airport.

➤ With flights always delayed or canceled, you wonder
why they bother to put out a schedule. Of course,
they need something to base their delays on.

➤ I was almost late getting here. We circled the airport for two hours. What made it difficult was
that we were in a bus.

America

➤ In America we produce more food than any other
country in the world . . . and more diets to keep
us from eating it.

➤ America—what a country! They lock up the jury
every night . . . and let the prisoner go home.

➤ America is the only country where you can borrow
a $10,000 down payment from a relative, get a
$60,000 first mortgage, a $30,000 second, and
be called a homeowner.

➤ American idealism often means being willing to
make any sacrifice that won't hurt business.

➤ America is the only place where the people demand
a speed limit of 55 and cars that will do 100.

➤ America is the only place where real estate developers bulldoze the trees, and then name the streets after them.

Bankruptcy

➤ Some business people are superstitious about bankruptcy. I know of one who won't read a book all the way through if he has to go through Chapter 11.

➤ I know another who won't watch football because he can't stand to see anything end up in the hands of a receiver.

➤ Paying off creditors after you've gone out of business is like making your car payments after the wreck.

➤ Paying off creditors after you've gone out of business is like leaving the TV set on after you've fallen asleep.

➤ The gods gave us fire and we invented the fire engine. They gave us ambition, and we invented bankruptcy.

➤ He was such a terrible businessman, he went bankrupt twice and didn't make a cent either time.

➤ Bankruptcy is a legal proceeding where you put your money in your pants pocket and give your coat to your creditors.

➤ He had a lot of nerve. He took a taxi to bankruptcy court and invited the driver in as a creditor.

➤ Three executives were fighting over the check at lunch. One said, "Let me take it, I can write it off on my taxes." Another said, "Let me pay, I can charge it to the company." The third said, "No, I'll take it—I'm filing for bankruptcy tomorrow."

Banks

➤ I think the reason banks have drive-up tellers is so the cars can see their real owners.

➤ I prefer automated tellers to the real ones. They usually have more personality.

➤ It's unfortunate that the person who writes the bank's advertising doesn't also approve the loans.

➤ Banks lend billions to Third World countries, but for us they chain down the pens.

➤ A banker is just a pawnbroker in a three-piece suit.

➤ A bank is an institution where you can borrow money if you can present sufficient evidence that you don't need it.

➤ Many smaller banks have gone through reorganization after discovering that they had more vice presidents than depositors.

➤ A South American dictator on his deathbed asked for six American bankers to be his pallbearers. He figured that since they'd carried him this long, they might as well finish the job.

➤ "A banker is a fellow who lends you his umbrella when the sun is shining and wants it back the minute it begins to rain." (Mark Twain)

Bills/Creditors

➤ I sent a customer a letter that said, "This bill is now one year old." He responded right away. He sent a note that said, "Happy Birthday."

➤ It's better to give than to lend . . . and it costs about the same.

➤ The best way to get deadbeats to pay you is to tell all their other creditors that they did.

➤ One customer haggled the price down at the time of the sale, and then never paid anyway. I asked him, "If you weren't going to pay, why'd you argue about the price for so long?" He said, "I didn't want you to lose too much."

➤ One's credit is the only commodity that becomes better the less it's used.

➤ How does credit work? A person who can't pay gets another person who can't pay to guarantee that the first one will pay.

➤ Debt is the certain outcome of uncertain income.

➤ "The two greatest stimulants in the world are youth and debt." (Benjamin Disraeli)

➤ "No man is impatient with his creditors." (Talmud)

Boss/Management

➤ It's not that our CEO has a big ego, but he was coming out of McDonald's and his head got stuck in the Golden Arch.

➤ I asked the boss what he wanted for Christmas and he said, "The usual . . . gold, frankincense, and myrrh."

➤ I had a boss once tell me, "You'll find a little something extra in your pay envelope this week." It was a pink slip.

➤ He's a tough boss. If you're five minutes late, he docks your pay. If you're five minutes early, he charges you rent.

➤ What does it mean to someone to report to a boss who gives them support, understanding, and respect? It usually means they're in the wrong office.

➤ She asked the boss if she could have a day off because it was her silver wedding anniversary. The boss said, "Do I have to put up with this every 25 years?"

➤ One employee complained to the boss when he was let go. "How can you fire me? I'm doing the work of three people." The boss said, "Tell me who the other two are and I'll fire them too!"

➤ In the high-tech industries, management has a language all its own. They don't tell people they're fired . . . they say they've been de-hired.

➤ She always gives her employees long vacations.
It's her way of discovering who she can do without.

➤ He's a very flexible boss. He allows me to come
in any time I want before nine, and leave any time
I want after five.

Bureaucracy

See "Government."

Business/Sales

➤ You know your business is in trouble when your
insurance company sends you just half a calendar.

➤ If I were to paint you a picture of last year's sales,
it would be a still life.

➤ We had to cut back at all levels. Even our CEO
is now forced to take his lunch with a domestic
chablis.

➤ If the economy is bouncing back, why are so many
of our customer's checks doing the same?

➤ After the way our sales went last year, I'm beginning to realize why all our new high-rise office
buildings have windows you can't open.

➤ This year's financial report is being brought to
you in color: red.

➤ This year, instead of giving our sales people
expense accounts to entertain clients, we may
give them gift certificates to McDonald's.

➤ When somebody went into our main store and asked for change of a twenty, we considered making them a partner.

➤ Someone called the store and asked what time we opened. We said, "What time can you make it?"

➤ Business is so quiet you can hear the overhead piling up.

➤ A corporation is an ingenious device for obtaining individual profit without individual responsibility.

➤ "When two men in a business always agree, one of them is unnecessary." (William Wrigley, Jr.)

Christmas (Parties, etc.)

➤ Looking around the room I see that the Christmas tree isn't the only thing that's lit up today.

➤ [Co worker] just doesn't understand the meaning of Christmas. He thinks the Three Wise Men were three guys who got out of the stock market at the right time.

➤ We considered giving each of the employees a unique kind of gift this year—batteries, toys not included.

➤ [Woman] still believes in Santa Claus. Anything to let her sit on a man's lap!

➤ My son [daughter] did a Christmas drawing showing two camels approaching the inn and one going in the opposite direction. He [she] said, "He's looking for a place to park."

Closing Lines

➤ I've always felt that presentations of this type should end on the same day as they begin . . . so I'll close now.

➤ If I've gotten my message across, it's my hope that some of you will leave here inspired . . . and the rest of you will at least wake up refreshed.

➤ It's said a good speech has a good beginning and a good ending, both of which are kept close together. Thank you.

➤ I want to thank you all for being such a fine audience . . . especially those of you who stayed awake the entire time.

➤ In closing, I'd like you to remember that it's not the speech that counts—but how quickly you end it. Thank you.

➤ I want to thank you for being an attentive audience. I appreciated your applause and your laughter . . . you showed very good judgement.

➤ A speech is like a love affair. Any fool can start it, but to end it requires considerable skill.

Competition

➤ Our competition obviously has a lot of customers who are willing to overlook little things . . . like service, prices, and reliability.

➤ People often ask how our competition can make money selling their products so cheaply. It's simple—they make their profits repairing those products.

➤ Everyone has the right to make mistakes, but [the competition] abuses the privilege.

➤ When their actual sales figures match their projections, it's strictly a coincidence.

➤ Talk about poor planning! By the time they finished putting up their new office building in the suburbs, the suburbs had moved 20 miles further out.

➤ They're in a great location. Just ten minutes from downtown . . . by phone.

➤ I understand [competitor] was out of the country for a while. He [she] was in Afganistan teaching the Russians to fight dirty.

➤ We spent ten years developing this product. It took us that long to steal the formula from [competitor].

➤ "Competition brings out the best in products and the worst in people." (David Sarnoff)

Computers

➤ Computers have saved our office millions of manhours. And we needed that time to correct all the computer-billing mistakes.

➤ Computers will take some getting used to. Remember when banks first started using automatic tellers, and you were a little hesitant about doing business with a cold machine? Then after a while you realized that the computer had more personality than most bank tellers.

➤ The expression "credit where credit is due" must have been started before there was computer billing.

➤ We had a tough day at our office. The computers went down and everybody had to learn to think all over again.

➤ What's the opposite of a computer nerd? Anybody who's had to live or work with one!

➤ One of our clerks was let go because of a new software program that enabled a computer to do everything he used to do. The sad part was, his wife went out and bought one.

Consultants

➤ A consultant is someone who will take your watch off your wrist and tell you what time it is.

➤ There's an old saying: If it ain't broke, don't fix it . . . unless you're a consultant.

➤ Why are consulting firms always called "associates"? Whom do they associate with, and who could stand it?

➤ A consultant is someone who is called in at the last minute to share the blame.

➤ An accountant is just a consultant hired by a successful person to explain to the government how he succeeded.

➤ A consultant is just an executive who can't find another job.

Conventions/Hotels

➤ A lot of people think that conventions are nothing but wine, women, and song—but I haven't heard any singing.

➤ I'm here with [boss]. You know how it is when you go on a trip . . . you always take something you don't need.

➤ Have you noticed that every year it costs less to fly here . . . and more to get to the airport?

➤ The hotel was a little nervous about booking our group. In the bathroom I noticed that the towels were chained down.

➤ I accidently left my electric toothbrush on all night . . . and now there's no enamel left in the bathroom.

➤ Our last annual conference was so successful that some people wanted to have another one the next week.

➤ I don't know if I would eat in the hotel restaurant. They accept cards from Diners Club, American Express, and Blue Cross.

➤ The coffee they serve is a blend . . . today's and yesterday's.

➤ The low point of the convention so far was when the hotel kitchen was cited by the United Nations for human rights violations.

➤ The prices are really something. I guess $50 for a meal for two isn't bad . . . but for continental breakfast?

➤ They change the rates every hour. I used up my expense allowance just sleeping.

➤ My room was so far from the front desk that by the time I got to my door, I owed two days rent.

➤ And what a room! It was the first time I ever had one where you had to tip the attendant.

➤ At the next convention, my name tag is going to use an alias.

➤ [Co-conventioneer] may have had a little bit too much to drink last night. Long after the party broke up, he was out in the parking lot, posing as a speed bump.

➤ He embarrassed us at the hotel. He was falling down at the front door so often, the staff thought he was a lawn ornament.

➤ "A conference is a gathering of important people who singly can do nothing, but together decide that nothing can be done." (Fred Allen)

Creditors

See: "Bills."

Doctors

See: "Health Care."

Economy/Inflation

➤ If the national debt gets any bigger, some of the larger industrial states may be repossessed.

➤ They say the economy is bouncing back . . . but so are our customers' checks.

➤ You know inflation is bad when you drop your wallet on the sidewalk and get arrested for littering.

➤ Most Americans drive last year's car, wear this year's clothes, and live on next year's income.

➤ I'm living so far beyond my income that you could almost say we're living apart.

➤ What used to cost $100 to buy now costs $500 to fix.

➤ At the current rate of inflation, dollars-to-donuts is no longer good odds.

➤ The salary we used to dream of is the one we can't live on today.

➤ Inflation is when nobody has enough money because everybody has too much money.

➤ Inflation is a lot like overeating . . . it feels good right up to the time when it's too late to correct it.

➤ A recession is a period in which you tighten your belt. In a depression, you have no belt to tighten. And when you have no pants to hold up, it's a panic.

➤ I'll try to keep my remarks brief, because I'd like to finish speaking before prices go up again.

➤ Economics is the study of how limited resources can best be made to serve unlimited wants.

➤ An economist is a person with the data to prove that all the confusion about what's going to happen isn't mere coincidence.

Education

➤ It's still possible to get a good high school education, but you have to go to college to get it.

➤ There are history students who can see "Gone with the Wind" with the added excitement of not knowing who's going to win the Civil War.

➤ Our high schools are turning out students who think Betsy Ross used to be the lead singer in the Supremes.

➤ Perhaps we should call a college education by another name: remedial high school.

➤ There are many advantages to having an education. If you couldn't sign your name you'd always have to pay cash.

➤ Many universities have become large athletic associations—where some studies are maintained for the benefit of the feeble-bodied.

➤ Education is the knowledge that enables you to insult somebody and call it repartee.

➤ Education is the ability to quote Shakespeare without crediting it to the Bible.

➤ "An educated man earns more. And it seldom takes more than ten years after graduating to get educated." (Washington Post)

Employees

➤ One employee went to his boss and said he demanded a raise because there were three other companies after him. The boss asked which three and he said, "The phone company, the gas company, and the finance company."

➤ These days when you tell employees they're spending too much time hanging around Mr. Coffee, you can expect they'll bring in Mr. Lawyer.

➤ You know your employees are discontented when you go to eat in the company cafeteria and across the door there's a band of white paper that says, "Sanitized For Your Protection."

➤ You know you've got a problem when you find out your controller is taking an extra-long coffee break . . . in Brazil.

➤ One way to make sure everyone gets to work on time would be to have 95 parking spaces for every 100 employees.

➤ Our controller has a thing about checkbooks. Once she starts one she can't put it down until she's finished.

➤ You know you've got employee relations problems when:

1. You have to ask Personnel to hire you a food taster.
2. The employees start referring to the parking lot as "the demilitarized zone."
3. The employees pledge that they won't be the first to use tactical nuclear weapons.
4. You find out your employees have developed first-strike nuclear capabilities.

EXECUTIVES

➤ He's our company's youngest executive, but the senior vice presidents try not to notice . . . except when he sends them memos written in crayon.

➤ When I was a junior executive, the senior VPs would always make sure I took part in their decision-making process. They even let me toss the coin.

➤ They even gave me my own special parking place. Of course, it was in [neighboring town].

➤ If this company adds any more executives, there'll be nobody left to do the work.

➤ I have some good news and some bad news. The good news is, the executive washroom is getting a shower installed. The bad news is, to cover the cost we're putting in pay toilets.

➤ An executive is someone who talks to visitors so the other employees can get the work done.

➤ An executive is someone who can take two hours for lunch without hindering production.

Exercise

➤ I love aerobics: my pulse starts racing, my heart pounds, I break out in a sweat—and that's just from watching the women [men].

➤ Usually when I feel like exercising, I lie down until the feeling goes away.

➤ There's a new kind of service very popular now with health-conscious people in [wealthy area] . . . valet jogging.

➤ If you resist any new form of exercise long enough, some expert will eventually tell you that it's actually bad for your health.

➤ Don't smoke, don't drink, eat simple foods, get plenty of sleep, and even if you don't live a long time, it will seem like a long time.

➤ "The only way to keep your health is to eat what you don't want, drink what you don't like, and do what you'd rather not." (Mark Twain)

Experience

➤ Experience is that wonderful knowledge that enables you to recognize a mistake when you make it again.

➤ Experience is the comb life gives you after you lose your hair.

➤ If we could sell experience for what it cost us, we'd all be very rich.

➤ Experience is generally what you get when you're expecting something better.

➤ Experience may be the best teacher, but it's often late to school.

➤ "We learn from experience that men never learn anything from experience." (George Bernard Shaw)

Farming

➤ A farm is a piece of land on which, if you work very hard, you make a lot of money . . . if you strike oil.

➤ A U.S. farmer is the only person who can lose money every year, live well, and die rich.

➤ Owning a farm is what a city person dreams of at 5 P.M., never at 5 A.M.

> These days a successful small farmer is one who sold the farm to a golf club.

> "Even if a farmer intends to loaf, he gets up in time to get an early start." (Edgar W. Howe)

> "Farming looks mighty easy when your plow is a pencil and you're a thousand miles from the cornfield." (Dwight Eisenhower)

Fund Raising

> The chairman called me three times to ask me to make this presentation. I finally told the operator I would accept the charges.

> I'm deeply touched by the turnout today . . . but not as deeply touched as you have been [will be].

> We're looking for people who have a love of checkbooks: once they start one they can't put it down until it's finished.

> Let's all give as generously as we report to the IRS.

> A woman said to a panhandler, "I never give money to anyone on the street." He said, "What shall I do, open an office?"

> When most of us start out in fund raising, we're wearing rose-colored glasses. But when we take them off, we find we're still in the red.

> Remember, it's better to give than to receive . . . and it usually costs less.

➤ We're only going to appeal to you one time . . . we're putting all our begs in one basket.

Government/Bureaucracy

➤ Asking the government for advice on how to run a business is like going to Howard Cosell for lessons in humility.

➤ If the ancient Egyptians had to put up with modern bureaucracy, they'd still be working on the pyramids.

➤ The business of a bureaucrat is delaying other people's business.

➤ I know the owner of a small firm who told his son he wanted him to share the business . . . but the government beat him to it.

➤ A government that's big enough to give you everything you want is big enough to take everything you've got.

➤ Congress is where someone gets up to speak and says nothing, nobody listens, and everybody disagrees.

➤ Every time Congress sets out to cut the budget, the knife slips and the taxpayers end up bleeding.

➤ One way to make sure that crime doesn't pay would be to have the government take it over and run it.

➤ If you think we've got too much government now, imagine what it would be like if we got as much as we're paying for.

➤ The government is making it harder than ever to stay in business. If you do something wrong you get fined, and if you do it right you get taxed.

➤ "In general, the art of government consists in taking as much money as possible from one party of the citizens to give it to the other." (Voltaire)

Health Care/Doctors

➤ The difference between an itch and an allergy is about $300 worth of tests.

➤ The single greatest feature that distinguishes humans from animals is the desire to take medicine.

➤ With medical costs so high, a lot of people have taken to using books to doctor themselves. So it's now possible to die of a misprint.

➤ In medical schools today it seems that before they teach doctors to check the patient's pulse, they teach them to check his credit rating.

➤ One hospital is being forced to take some unusual measures to cut costs. For instance, now they have patients make their own beds. When you check in they give you a tool box and some wood.

➤ They only charged me $20 for X-rays, but they talked me into a set of wallet-sized prints and two eight-by-tens.

➢ The nurse was very attractive. When she took my temperature she subtracted ten percent for personality.

➢ Fortunately, my doctor doesn't believe in unnecessary surgery. He won't operate unless he absolutely needs the money.

➢ My health insurance guarantees that if I'm hospitalized, I'll be provided with a room with a semi-private bed.

➢ My doctor put me on my feet in no time. To pay his bill I had to sell my car.

➢ Two burglars broke into my doctor's office . . . and he charged them for a visit.

➢ Personally, I always pay my medical bills promptly . . . as an incentive for my doctor to keep me alive.

➢ "The art of medicine consists in amusing the patient while nature cures the disease." (Voltaire)

Hecklers/Hostile Audience

➢ I have great admiration for your open-mindedness in inviting me to speak . . . and for my courage in accepting.

➢ You'll notice that I move around the room a lot when I speak. This is because it gives me closer contact with the audience . . . and it's harder to hit a moving target.

➤ [After silence at an open question:] Did E. F. Hutton just speak?

Comebacks to Hecklers

➤ I've only got today to make a fool of myself . . . you've got the rest of your life.

➤ I don't know what I'd do without you . . . but I'm willing to try.

➤ I came here with a terrible toothache, but compared to you it's a pleasure.

➤ Why not call me . . . so I can hang up on you.

➤ She always speaks her mind. The trouble is, it limits her conversation.

➤ I don't care if you walk out on me . . . it's when you walk toward me that I worry.

Hotels

See "Conventions."

Insurance

➤ One agent who was very proud of the policy he had just sold asked the client, "Now what do you think you'd get if your business burned down tomorrow?" The client said, "About five to ten years."

➤ One claims investigator came back to the office and reported that the cause of a suspicious fire was friction . . . from rubbing a $200,000 policy on a $100,000 house.

➤ An insurance saleman is someone who first persuades you to apply for a policy because you're going to die at any minute, then won't issue it until they're sure you're in good health.

➤ An insurance salesman sold me a retirement policy. If I keep up the payments for ten years, he can retire.

➤ Life insurance is like most of the good things in life . . . the older you get, the more it costs.

➤ They say that one of the greatest pleasures of growing old is freedom from life insurance salesmen.

➤ Some of these new accident policies are so attractive, a person almost can't afford to die a natural death.

➤ One woman insisted she would never carry any life insurance. She said, "When I die, I want it to be a sad day for everyone."

Introductions

➤ The last time she spoke she had the audience glued to their seats . . . which was a clever idea.

➤ [Speaker] is our only speaker. The rest of the program is entertainment.

➤ Most people don't drink coffee during her after-dinner speeches. They're afraid it'll keep them awake.

➤ They say the duty of a toastmaster is to be so dull that the succeeding speakers will seem brilliant by contrast. [pause] How am I doing?

➤ [Speaker] was a little upset when I got up and left during his last presentation. It was unintentional . . . I sometimes walk in my sleep.

➤ Our next speaker is a master of repartee. You know what repartee is . . . that's what you didn't say the last time and will have forgotten by the next time.

➤ Our discussion of [subject] has been very enlightening so far. I'm still confused, but on a much higher plane.

➤ I'm your emcee. That's the person who alibis for the last speaker and exaggerates for the next one.

➤ Scientists say that the sense of hearing is considerably dulled by eating—which is nature's way of protecting us against after-dinner speakers. Fortunately, you won't need such protection from [speaker].

➤ "It usually takes more than three weeks to prepare a good impromptu speech." (Mark Twain)

Investments

➤ You know you've got the wrong broker when you order 100 shares of IBM and he asks you how to spell it.

➤ A friend of mine lost a lot of money in a pyramid scheme . . . her broker ran off to Egypt.

➤ I know a financial advisor whose luck was so bad, his portfolio dropped 50 percent in one day . . . and this was a Saturday!

➤ A lot of people bought gold as a hedge against inflation. When interest rates went down, a lot of hedges got trimmed.

➤ There's only one sure-fire method for getting a small fortune out of the stock market. Go in with a large fortune.

➤ When he talks about his broker, you don't know if he means stock or pawn.

➤ I expect to do very well in the market this month . . . my broker's on vacation.

➤ With my investments, I sleep like a baby—all night I sleep an hour, then get up and cry for an hour.

➤ Investing in stocks isn't much different than buying a lottery ticket—except in the lottery, the odds are better.

➤ Remember, the sound, secure investments of today are the tax write-offs of tomorrow.

➤ The basic necessities of life today are food, clothing, and tax shelters.

➤ When my broker says the institutions are buying, I have to wonder if he means the directors or the inmates.

➤ My broker has learned to do one thing really well after ten years in the business . . . apologize.

➢ Being your own broker can give you the same result as do-it-yourself plumbing . . . you don't have to be in your tub to take a bath.

➢ Attitudes in America are changing. It used to be that married people stayed together until the children were grown. Now they stay together until the IRA matures.

➢ Money isn't everything, but it's a long way ahead of whatever comes next.

➢ There was a time when a fool and his money were soon parted. Now it happens to everyone.

IRS/Taxes

➢ Professional tax planning can save every taxpayer time. Those into shelters might save five to ten years.

➢ Creativity is what you use when you fill out your tax return. When you explain it to the IRS, that's innovation.

➢ Being a tax advisor is a tricky business. The tax laws change more often than George Steinbrenner changes managers.

➢ The tax forms prove that it's possible to get wounded by a blank.

➢ If Patrick Henry thought that taxation without representation was tyranny, he should see it today with representation.

➤ One business owner showed up for an IRS audit with 400 little black diaries all filled with expenses. But it didn't help. They asked him what business he was in and he told them, "I sell little black diaries."

Lawyers

➤ Remember the story of the lawyer who fell overboard at sea. A shark swam toward him but turned away at the last second: professional courtesy.

➤ A criminal lawyer blew a case, and the defendant, who was going to the electric chair, asked for advice. The lawyer said, "Don't sit down."

➤ Where there's a will, there's a way. Where there's no will, there are lawyers.

➤ A lawyer is one who protects us against robbery by taking away the temptation.

➤ A divorce lawyer is like a fight referee who winds up with the purse.

➤ My attorney is brilliant. He can look at a contract and tell you in a minute if it's oral or written.

➤ A jury is a group of 12 people selected to decide who has the better lawyer.

Management

See "Boss."

Opening Lines

> I'm going to speak, and you're hopefully going to listen. If you finish before I do, please raise your hand.

> They sent a limo out to the airport to pick me up. Unfortunately, I was at the Greyhound bus station.

> Last night when I reviewed my presentation, I made an effort to eliminate anything on the dull side. So in conclusion . . .

> Our work to improve [cause] will probably never end. Don't worry—the same won't be said of my speech today.

> I'll be happy to answer any questions you might have when I finish my speech. Just don't ask, "Why did you bother to show up?"

> A lot of you are probably in the "who's who" of this business. I'm more in the category of "who's he?"

> I guess some of you have heard me speak before, so you came early and got a good seat—near the door.

> Accustomed as I am to public speaking, I know the futility of it.

> It's a pleasure to speak to the members of [organization]: deep in tradition, deep in history, deep in debt.

➤ The last time I spoke to a group like this, the chairwoman offered me a small honorarium, which I declined. She was very happy—she said she would put the money in their "improvement" fund. I asked her what that was and she said, "We're hoping to save enough so that next time we can have a better speaker."

➤ I feel privileged to be speaking to you in this beautiful auditorium. The word auditorium has an interesting origin. It comes from the Latin word audio, to hear, and taurus—the bull.

➤ When I asked the chairman how long I should speak, he said, "Take as long as you want—we all leave at 9:30."

After banquet:
➤ I'm standing here because I've heard that the only way to stay awake during an after-dinner speech is to deliver it.

➤ I was a little puzzled by what [chairperson] said to me just before I came up here. She said, "Shall we let them enjoy their dessert and coffee a little longer, or shall we have your speech now?"

After applause:
➤ Sure . . . but will you still respect me in the morning?

➤ Thank you. To applaud like that at the beginning of a speech is truly an act of faith. If you applaud in the middle, it's an act of hope. And if you applaud at the end. . . .

After flattering introduction:
➤ After that introduction, I can hardly wait to hear what I'm going to say.

➤ I wish my mother and father were here to hear that introduction. My father might have enjoyed it. My mother might have believed it.

When many seats are empty:
➤ This must be a very wealthy audience. I see everybody bought two or three seats.

➤ I'm not disappointed by the size of the crowd. I'd just like to know who heard me speak before and squealed?

➤ This reminds me of when I used to help my uncle on his farm. If I took the trouble to haul a load of feed down to the barn lot, and only one or two cows showed up instead of 50, I still fed the one or two. But of course, I didn't give them the whole bag.

Optimists

➤ An optimist is a person who believes that what's going to be will be postponed.

➤ An optimist is someone who can always see the bright side of somebody else's troubles.

➤ A pessimist is just an optimist with more information.

➤ A friend came to an optimist and said, "My business is bankrupt, my house is going to be foreclosed on, and I don't have a cent coming in." He told him, "You can be thankful you aren't one of your creditors."

➤ Those people who always say "Can't complain" just aren't trying hard enough.

Philosophy

➤ Civilization is a state of affairs where nothing can be done without first securing financing.

➤ Advice is like medicine: the correct dosage can work wonders, but an overdose can be fatal.

➤ When you meet a person who believes that poverty and hard work are good for character, you know you're talking to someone with money.

➤ A profession is something you study for years to get into, and then spend the rest of your life trying to earn enough to get out of.

➤ When money talks, hardly anyone pays attention to the grammar.

➤ When you get something for nothing, you just haven't been billed yet.

➤ Reputation is character minus what you've been caught doing.

➤ One reason that crime doesn't pay is that when it does, it's always called by a more respectable name.

➤ Poise is the ability to be ill at ease naturally.

➤ After you hear two eyewitness accounts of the same auto accident, you begin to wonder about history.

Phone Company

➤ The reason they put a zip code map in the phone book is so that if your call doesn't go through, you can write.

➤ The phone company has made a lot of contributions to society—for one, they gave Superman a place to change clothes.

➤ The phone company claims to have fewer problems than the other utilities. That's only because there are no nuclear phones.

➤ It used to be that the strongest guy in the neighborhood was the one that could tear a phone book in half. Now it's the one who can do that with his phone bill.

Politics

➤ Looking at the two candidates, I'm thankful . . . only one of them can get elected.

➤ He's a shrewd politician. He always sits to the left of Republicans, to the right of Democrats, and in front of any cameras.

➤ I intend to live up to all my promises if elected . . . but I'd appreciate it if you didn't take notes.

➤ Too often, elections are influenced not so much by what the candidate stands for as by what the voter falls for.

➤ Politics is the art of getting funds from the rich and votes from the poor, by promising to protect each group from the other.

➤ A conservative is someone who doesn't think anything should be done for the first time.

➤ A conservative is someone who acts impulsively after thinking for a long time.

➤ I'm a Democrat because my father was one and his father was one. But if my father had been a bank robber and my grandfather was a horse thief . . . I'd be a Republican.

➤ Politics is the art of looking for trouble, finding it everywhere, diagnosing it incorrectly, and applying the wrong solutions.

➤ If you want to learn about your family history, run for office . . . and the press will tell you everything.

➤ A statesman is a successful politician who died.

➤ "America is the only country where you can go on TV and kid the politicians . . . and they can go on TV and kid the people." (Groucho Marx)

➤ "Political ability is the ability to foretell what is going to happen tomorrow, next week, next month, and next year . . . and the ability afterward to explain why it didn't happen." (Winston Churchill)

Real Estate

➤ People who got into the real estate business because they heard it was a gold mine are learning that all that glitters is not sold.

➤ In real estate, you have to be careful when opportunity comes knocking. It might damage the front door.

➤ You know you've got a questionable property when the termites refer to it as "junk food."

➤ The property looked a little shaky to me—the termites were wearing crash helmets.

➤ When the wind blew the termites had to hold hands to keep the building from falling down.

➤ I think that building needed a paint job. There was graffiti on it about Calvin Coolidge.

➤ The landlord was arrested and charged with robbing people who were not his tenants.

➤ My new house has wall-to-wall carpeting, wall-to-wall windows, and back-to-wall financing.

➤ A tenant who was moving out of his apartment asked the landlord where he could buy 20,000 cockroaches. When the landlord asked why, he told him, "Because the lease said I have to leave the premises exactly the way I found them."

➤ Sometimes the descriptions in the real estate catalogues can be misleading. One couple who had

their house up for sale changed their mind after
they read the listing—it seemed to be just the
place they were looking for.

➤ The house was in a very quiet neighborhood . . .
it was kind of like a cemetery with lights.

➤ These 15-year mortgages mean that, if you work on
the place every weekend for the life of the loan,
you might just be able to get it in shape to sell.

[Real estate salesperson:]
➤ A wrong number called and asked if he sold mater-
nity clothes. He said, "No . . . but you're going
to need a bigger house."

Retirement

➤ He goes back a long way with the company. When
he first started here, Xerox made copies by hand.

➤ Why is it when you retire and time is no longer
so important, they give you a watch?

➤ We were going to give [retiree] the traditional gold
watch, but when they showed it to me, I liked it
so much that I had it bronzed.

➤ In a very moving ceremony on [retiree]'s last day,
we had his coffee cup bronzed.

➤ He thinks the worst thing about retirement is
that he'll have to drink coffee on his own time.

➤ The worst thing about retirement is that she'll
have to drink coffee on her own time.

> I remember when he first started in the company—
at the bottom. He had the only office where you
had to tip the attendant.

[Bald retiree:]
> God made lots of heads. Those he was ashamed
of he covered with lots of hair.

Roasts

> In many ways, he's been like a son to me: ungrate-
ful, arrogant, disrespectful . . .

> Her ancestors came over on the Mayflower. For-
tunately, immigration laws are now much stricter.

> He has a lot in common with Johnny Carson.
Carson appears on TV every night . . . and he
watches a lot.

> If you've ever had lunch with her, you'll understand
why when she was sick last winter, she got a get
well card from McDonald's.

[Messy desk:]
> He was going to clean off his desk one day, but
he was afraid it would upset the ecology.

[Ugly:]
> She wasn't the cutest teenager. Her parents threw
away her graduation picture and framed the negative.

[Ugly:]
> They tried to bronze his baby shoes . . . while he
was wearing them.

[Handsome:]
➤ The women in his office voted him most likely to succeed . . . with anyone!

[Boss:]
➤ He doesn't read Fortune . . . but he eats a lot of their cookies.

[Woman boss:]
➤ She was late arriving back to town. The airport had her broomstick in a holding pattern.

[Milquetoast:]
➤ You wouldn't know it to look at him, but he once worked as a bouncer . . . in a salad bar.

[Tough:]
➤ When he was in the military he had an embarrassing accident and lost a vital organ. But he was so tough, he grew another one.

[Smoker:]
➤ If he went to a meeting of the American Cancer Society, he'd ask to sit in the smoking section. . . . He's trying to quit. He's in phase 1 — he's stopped buying. . . . In our office we have a saying: Where there's smoke, there's [roastee].

[Overweight:]
➤ He thinks he's in good shape, but when he went for a physical, the doctor had to drill for blood.

[Short:]
➤ He's not a big man. In our annual report, his picture is actual size.

[Bald:]
➤ On his driver's license under "hair color" it says "Does not apply." . . . His high school class voted him "Most Likely to Recede."

[Bad dresser:]
➤ He told me that whenever he's down in the dumps, he buys a new suit. I was wondering where he got them!

[Drinker:]
➤ Later on he'll take questions from the floor . . . but he'll need a few more drinks to get there.

[Drinker:]
➤ She knows her capacity but she gets drunk before she reaches it.

[Married:]
➤ His wife wants to fly to Hawaii for a second honeymoon . . . and she wants him to drive her to the airport.

[Cheap:]
➤ You can always recognize him at lunch—he's the one sitting with his back to the check. . . . He wouldn't offer to buy a round of drinks at an AA meeting. . . . He bought his daughter a dollhouse with a mortgage on it.

Sales

See "Business."

Salesmen/Saleswomen

➤ An Arab returned home to the desert after a vacation in the United States carrying a pair of skis. His friend asked him, "What impressed you most about America?" He said, "The salesmen."

➤ And to think that when he was in the Army they asked him if he wanted a commission and he said, "No, I'd rather work for straight salary."

➤ He once sold two milking machines to a farmer with only one cow . . . and took the cow as a down payment.

➤ When a salesperson tells me I can buy something for a song, I watch out for the accompaniment.

➤ Selling is a little like hog calling—it isn't the noise you make, it's the appeal in your voice.

Sports

[Tennis:]
➤ I was a little disappointed when I found out that 15-love wasn't what I thought it was . . . In tennis, love means zero—reminds me of last night.

[Jogging:]
➤ Thanks to jogging, more people than ever before are dying in perfect health.

[Skiing:]
➤ He had a skiing accident in the mountains, and when the rescue party found him and said they

were from the Red Cross, he told them, "Sorry,
I already gave this year."

[Golf:]

➢ Golf—that's a lot of walking, broken up by dis-
appointment and bad arithmetic.

➢ He plays golf in the low 70s. He won't go out if
it gets any colder.

➢ He hits so many balls in the water, the fish are
going to start charging a green fee.

➢ When he addresses the ball, it's to whom it may
concern.

➢ She's won more golf games with her pencil than
she has with a putter or driver.

➢ Some of you may have seen me teamed with Jack
Nicklaus at the pro-am golf tournament. Jack
won't let anyone else carry his bag.

Stock Market

See "Investments."

Taxes

See "IRS."

Television

➢ TV permits you to be entertained in your living
room by people you wouldn't ordinarily let into
your house.

➢ In our parents' day you could see two movies for ten cents in any theater. Now you get the same two movies on a $500 TV set.

➢ Have you ever seen the Playboy Channel? It's still not perfected . . . but they're working on a fold-out TV screen.

➢ I got a call from some television people last week and they offered me a good deal, so . . . I've decided to renew my subscription to *TV Guide*.

➢ A television audience is a lot of people with nothing to do watching a lot of people doing it.

➢ "Television is chewing gum for the eyes." (Frank Lloyd Wright)

Unions

➢ When I was vacationing in the Southwest I saw my first rattlesnake. One of the local people said, "Watch out! If you get too close, it'll strike." And I said, "Good lord, do these things have unions, too?"

➢ A woman used to go to a doctor to see if she could have children. Now she consults her union contract.

➢ My father always told me, "Learn a trade so you'll be able to go out on strike."

➢ A retired union man came back to apply for a part-time job. The boss said, "How many years of experience do you have?" He said, "Sixty years." The boss said, "How can you have 60 years experience if you're only 59 years old?" He said, "I put in a lot of overtime."

➤ Labor and management both agree that time is money, but they can't agree on how much.

U.S. Cities/States

[Boston:]

➤ There's an old saying—if you hear an owl hoot "whom" instead of "who," he was probably born and educated in Boston.

➤ "We say the cows laid out Boston. Well, there are worse surveyors." (Ralph Waldo Emerson)

[California:]

➤ I was stopped by the California highway patrol—on suspicion of driving an American car.

➤ Where else does the board of directors choose a CEO based on his astrological sign?

➤ The heavy rains in winter cause a lot of problems. I got a ticket for going through a red light . . . and I was in a house at the time.

[Beverly Hills:]

➤ This is a pretty rich community. The unemployment office has valet parking.

[San Francisco:]

➤ On Fisherman's Wharf sometimes you can hardly walk down the street because there are hundreds of people crowding all over the sidewalk—and those are just the ones selling souvenirs. . . . I love to go

to Candlestick Park—even if it is the only stadium
in America where the fans are colder than the beer.

[Las Vegas:]
> I'm feeling optimistic. A friend of mine left here
last month with $20,000. Of course, he came with
$50,000.

> I once gambled away my car in Las Vegas . . . and
boy, were those Hertz people mad.

> Last time I was here I only made mental bets . . .
and I nearly lost my mind.

> It's nice to be at [hotel]. You can't beat the service,
the people, or the slot machines.

> This is the only city where the Western Union
office has preprinted messages for sending home
for money.

> This is the only place where you can see a woman
in a mink coat, covered with diamonds, standing
at the slot machine counting nickels.

[New York City:]
> When I got to New York I was told I could get an
excellent room for just $30 a night. But the room
was in New Jersey.

> In most towns, a stranger might come up to you
on the street and ask you what time it is. In New
York they'll just steal your watch.

> In New York they no longer give anyone the key
to the city . . . they send over someone to tell you
how to pick the lock.

➤ In front of my hotel I asked a guy if he wanted to share a cab. He said, "Okay . . . you take the tires, I'll take the battery."

[St. Louis (or Milwaukee):]
➤ A lot of people think this is a big beer-drinking town. That's not true. Last night I noticed that people were just packed into the local Baskin-Robbins. Flavor-of-the-Month was malt liquor.

[Seattle:]
➤ I understand that here in Seattle they have a saying: "My god, is it still raining?"

➤ At the local Baskin-Robbins, Flavor-of-the-Month is mildew.

➤ I called a friend here to check on the weather and he said, "It's not bad. Last week it only rained twice—once for three days and once for four days."

[Texas:]
➤ I love Texas . . . where they refer to Paul Revere as "the guy who had to run for help."

➤ Texas—where people do more business by accident than Wall Street does on purpose.

➤ A Texan died and went to heaven, and St. Peter greeted him at the gate and said, "Where're you from?" The man said, "Texas." St. Peter said, "Well, come on in . . . but you aren't going to be satisfied."

[Washington, D.C.:]
➤ It's a funny city. One week you're on the cover of *Time*, the next week you're doing it.

➤ Until I spent a summer in Washington, D.C.,
I never understood the true meaning of capital
punishment.

➤ It's great to be in Washington, D.C.—where the
skeletons in the closets are ashamed of the people
who live in the houses.

➤ "Washington is a city of Northern charm and
Southern efficiency." (John F. Kennedy)

Women in Business

➤ To get ahead in business today, a woman is
expected to look like a girl, behave like a lady,
think like a man, and work like a dog.

➤ The businesswoman today has to be twice as good
as a man. Fortunately, that's not hard.

➤ They say diamonds are a girl's best friend and
a dog is man's best friend. Now you know which
sex has more sense.

➤ One executive called his secretary into his office
and said, "Just because I make an occasional pass
at you, where did you get the idea that you could
do as you please around the office?" She said, "From
my attorney."

➤ Funny—I've never heard of a man being asked
how he combines marriage with a career.

➤ A female executive is a person who can mismanage
as badly as a man, only she gets blamed for it.

CHAPTER 7

Stories to Make a Point

Quirks of Accountants

➢ A company was trying to hire a new accountant and had narrowed the field down to three candidates to be interviewed. The first came in and they asked him, "How much is two plus two?" He said, "Four." They said "Thank you," and called in the next one. She was also asked, "How much is two plus two?" She said, "Four point zero." They said, "Thanks," and called in the final person. They asked again, "How much is two plus two?" He said, "How much do you want it to be?" They said, "You're hired!"

➢ A couple of tax accountants were trying to visit the grave of a former co-worker who had recently died, but they couldn't find it anywhere in the

cemetery. One finally said to the other, "Do you
think he put it in his wife's name?"

➢ From his first days with this firm, Smith has had
a strange habit. Every morning when he arrived he
would open the middle drawer of his desk, take
out a folded piece of paper, unfold it, read it, and
then fold it up again and put it back in the drawer.
Then he would start work. He did this every day
for months, until finally my curiosity got the best
of me, and one night after he left I went and opened
that drawer. The folded paper was the only thing
in there. I unfolded it and looked. There it was
written, in his own handwriting, "The debit side
is the one nearest the window."

Taking Good Advice

➢ I knew someone who had lost his life savings in
the commodities market. He was crushed and about
to take his own life. As he stood at the window
of his hotel room, he heard a voice say, "Don't
jump!" He was startled. He said, "Why not? I've
lost everything!" The voice said, "Borrow $100.
Call your broker, and buy soybeans." So he did as
he was told and that very day the price of soybeans
quadrupled. That night the voice said "Reinvest it
all in more soybeans." He did, and the price shot
up again. This happened every day for several weeks,
until the man had close to $50,000. Then the voice
said, "Stop now—that's all I can do for you." But
he couldn't resist trying soybeans a little longer—
and within a couple of days he had lost everything
again. He was totally crushed. He went back to
the hotel and stood at the window. He said aloud,

"I'm broke again—what should I do now?" The voice said, "Jump out the window."

You Won't Be Hearing Any Bull

➤ I recall a friend of mine who wanted to board her horse for a while. The first farmer she asked said he would keep it at $25 a day, plus he would keep the manure. My friend thought that was too high and went to another farmer. His price was $20 a day plus the manure. Then she went to a third farmer who asked just $5 a day. My friend said, "Why didn't you ask for the manure, too?" The farmer said, "At $5 a day, there won't be any!"

Career Expectations

➤ You may be familiar with the story of the man who brought his dog to a nightclub. The dog went straight to the piano and started playing a medley of popular songs. The manager of the club was amazed. He said to the dog's owner, "If you handle him right, you could make a fortune with an act like this." The owner just shook his head and said, "Naah, it'll never happen. He wants to be a doctor."

These Are Changing Times

➤ A successful business owner was scolding his lazy son. He said, "When I was your age, I worked 16 hours a day in this business." The son said, "And I appreciate it, Dad. If it hadn't been for your persistence and hard work . . . I might have had to do that myself."

Character Is Reflected in Actions, Not Words

➢ A truck driver stopped at a roadside diner to eat.
He got a hamburger, a cup of coffee, and a piece
of pie. As he was about to start eating, three rough-
looking guys in leather jackets pulled up on motor-
cycles and came inside. One grabbed his hamburger
and ate it. The second one drank his coffee, and
the other took his pie. The truck driver didn't say a
word. He got up, paid the cashier, and went out. One
of the bikers said to the cashier, "He's not much
of a man, is he?" She said, "He's not much of a
driver, either. He just ran his truck over three motor-
cycles."

Clarity Means Getting to the Point

➢ I remember arriving late to a conference in
Washington, D.C. I asked a woman coming out
of the auditorium, "Has the congressman begun
speaking yet?" The woman said, "Yes, he's been
speaking for half an hour." I said, "What is he
talking about?" The woman said, "I don't know,
he hasn't said yet."

Commitment Is Easy When Nothing's at Stake

➢ A young man very nervously approached his girl-
friend's father one evening and said, "Sir, I have
to ask you something very important. I was wondering how you would feel about, er. . . ." The father
interrupted and said, "Why, of course! You want
to marry my daughter? You're a fine young man,
you come from a good family; I'd be happy to give
you my blessing." But the boy said, "That's not it,

sir. You see, I had a car payment due next week, and if I don't come up with $100 right away, they're going to repossess the car. So I was wondering if. . . ." The father said, "Absolutely not! I hardly know you!"

Commitment Requires Some Sacrifice

➢ When I played basketball in my senior year of high school, I sat on the bench all season long. It looked like I was never going to get into a game. Then in the last game of the season, against our archrivals, we were losing by one point with just one minute left and the coach called my name. I jumped up and ran over for instructions and he said, "We can't stop the clock—we've run out of time-outs. Go in there and get hurt!"

Communication Is Often Difficult

➢ How many of us have gone through this scenario when trying to reach someone on the phone?
First thing in the morning: "He hasn't come in yet."
Later: "I expect him any minute."
Then: "He just called and said he'd be a little late."
Later: "He came in for a minute, but he stepped away from his desk."
Then: "He's gone to lunch."
Later: "I expect him back any minute."
You try again: "He hasn't come back yet. Can I take a message?"
Then: "He's somewhere in the building. His coat is here."
Later: "He went out again. I don't know when he'll be back."
Finally: "No, he's gone for the day."

The Value of Compromise

➤ A salesman had received a large Christmas bonus before going away on vacation, and when he got back his friends asked him what he'd done with the money. He said, "Well, my wife wanted one of those giant screen TVs, but I wanted a new car. So we bought the TV, but we compromised . . . we keep it in the garage."

Concessions Can Be Meaningless

➤ A criminal with a long record of convictions was being sentenced once more. The judge said, "You've been found guilty on two counts, and I'm sentencing you to the maximum on each one—consecutive life terms." The prisoner burst into tears. The judge saw this and softened a bit, and said, "Okay, maybe I'm being a bit harsh. You don't have to serve consecutive life terms." The prisoner stopped crying and the judge said, "I hereby cut your sentence in half."

Be Wary in Extending Credit

➤ An executive went into an office supplies store, rushed up to the owner, and said, "I understand my office manager has owed you on a typewriter for three years now." The owner said, "Yes—have you come to settle the account?" The executive said, "No—I'd like to buy one on the same terms."

Cultural Differences Are Not So Great As They Seem

➤ A small spaceship crash-landed in New York City, right opposite the famous Stage Delicatessen. An alien managed to get out and started checking the damage to his ship. While he was doing this, he noticed the bagels in the window of the delicatessen. He went inside and said, "Can I have one of those wheels for my spaceship?" The deli clerk said, "Those aren't wheels, they're bagels—you eat them." The spaceman didn't believe him. The clerk said, "Go ahead, try one." The alien slowly took a bite and then said, "You know, these wouldn't be bad with cream cheese."

Customer Relations—You Can't Be All Things to All People

➤ A restaurant prided itself on being able to fill any order for food, no matter how exotic. In fact, they offered $1,000 to anyone who could order something that they didn't serve. One day a man came in and told the waiter, "I'd like an order of walrus ears on a bun." Five minutes later the waiter came back and handed him $1,000 dollars. The man said, "Aha—no walrus ears, eh?" The waiter said, "No, we've got plenty of them—we just ran out of buns."

Customer Service Is a Difficult Task

➤ A man ordered a dozen roses to be sent to his wife on her birthday. When the roses arrived, there were only ten. He called up the florist, very angry, and said, "I bought a dozen roses and you only sent ten!" The florist said, "Don't get excited, that's part of our service. Two were wilted, so we saved your wife the trouble of throwing them away."

➤ A man went into an exclusive clothing store to buy a suit. The salesman asked him for his name, occupation, educational background, hobbies, religion, and political party. When the man asked why he wanted all that information, the salesman said, "Sir, we don't just sell you a suit. We make a suit that's exactly right for you. We analyze your personality and your background. We search the world for the kind of sheep that produces just the wool that your mood and character require. The wool is processed according to a special formula that reflects your personality. Then it's woven in a part of the world where the climate is most favorable to your temperament. After a series of preliminary fittings, we style a suit. Then—" The other man said, "Wait a minute. I need this suit for a wedding tomorrow afternoon." The salesman shrugged and said, "Don't worry, you'll have it."

➤ I remember the airline passenger who found a bug in the food he was served on the plane. After arriving home, he wrote an angry letter to the airline and got a quick reply. It said, "Dear Sir: Your letter was a source of great concern to us. We have never before received a complaint of this nature and will do everything possible to guarantee that such an incident never happens again." The man was satisfied with this until he noticed another slip of paper fall out of the envelope. It said, "Send this guy the bug letter."

Dishonesty Doesn't Pay

➤ A man traveling on vacation in Europe opened his wallet and found that somehow, before he left home, someone had slipped him an obviously fake $15 bill. He thought it would be easy enough to pass off on some European shopkeeper, so he went

into a store in a little town and bought something
for one dollar. He paid with the $15 bill. The shop-
keeper just looked at it, nodded, and gave him
his change—two seven-dollar bills.

Employees Are Hard to Satisfy

➤ The CEO called a meeting of all the employees in
the company and made the announcement they
all had been dreading. He said, "The rumor that's
been circulating for the past year is true. On the
first of next month, the whole plant will change over
to full automation." A loud rumble went through
the crowd, but the CEO silenced it right away. He
said, "But don't worry. Not a single person will
be laid off. You're going to keep your full salaries
and benefits as before. Everyone will be expected
to appear for work on Wednesday of each week—
Wednesday only." The crowd became silent. Then
a voice called out, "What? *Every* Wednesday?"

Exceptions Can Always Be Made

➤ A friend of mine arrived late to a conference in
New York because his plane had been held up trying
to land at Kennedy airport. When he finally got
to his hotel, they had given away the room he had
reserved because the hotel was full. He pleaded
with them to find him another room, but they
told him it was impossible. He said, "Look, if the
president came here right now and asked for a
room, you'd find him one, wouldn't you?" The manager said, "Well, if it was the president, I suppose
we could." My friend said, "Good. The president
isn't coming. Let me have his room."

Too Many Executives

➤ The new vice president was bragging about his promotion until one co-worker couldn't stand it anymore. His friend said, "Vice presidents are a dime a dozen today. Why, my supermarket even has a vice president in charge of peas." The other guy couldn't believe it, so he called the supermarket and asked for the vice president in charge of peas. The voice on the phone said, "Canned or frozen?"

You Don't Have to Live Up to Others' Expectations

➤ An old couple went to a crowded hotel and asked for a room. The clerk told them the place was filled up except for the honeymoon suite, but he could put them in there. The husband said, "The honeymoon suite! We've been married forty years!" The clerk said, "Look, if I give you the main ballroom, it doesn't mean you have to dance."

The Value of Practical Experience

➤ Last year my nephew's third-grade class was studying the solar system. The teacher let each child choose the topic he wanted to do a report on. One of my nephew's classmates took Mars, one took the moon, but he chose the planet Earth. When his friends asked him why, he said, "Because it's the only one I've visited."

Expert Advice Is Not Always Necessary

➤ A friend of mine had an investment counselor who would always say, "Never ever take any action without consulting me first." After the last stock market crash my friend called and said, "You've constantly told me that you would advise me of the best action to take. So how shall I act now?" The counselor said, "Act broke."

Don't Pay Attention to Flattery

➤ Two friends who hadn't seen each other in a while met on the street one day. One said, "What have you done to your hair? It's terrible, it looks like a wig." The other said, "It is a wig." The first then said, "Really? You could never tell."

Difficulties of Fund Raising

➤ A panhandler knocked on the door of a house and asked for something to eat. The woman who answered said, "I'll give you something to eat if you'll clean my yard first." The bum said, "Lady, I asked for a donation, not a transaction."

➤ A society matron was stopped by a panhandler as she was coming out of a big charity ball. When he asked her for a dollar she said, "I spent $200 for a ticket tonight, $2,000 for this dress, and on top of that I'm exhausted from dancing. How dare you ask me for money after I did all that for you!"

➤ When a fund raiser approached his town's tight-wad millionaire, the rich woman took the offensive. She said, "Look, I've got a 90-year-old mother in the hospital, a widowed sister with five kids, and two brothers who owe the IRS a fortune." The fund raiser was apologetic. He said, "I had no idea you were stuck with so many family debts." The rich woman said, "I'm not. So you think I'll give money to strangers when I won't even help my own relatives?"

➢ I remember the strongman at a carnival back in my childhood. As his final trick, he squeezed the juice from a lemon with his hands and then offered $100 to anyone who could squeeze another drop out of it. A frail little old lady came forward and tried it. With a tremendous effort, she squeezed one more drop from the lemon. The strongman said, "That's amazing. What's the secret of your strength?" She said, "Oh, for 30 years I was treasurer of (your organization)."

Government Restraints Make Things Difficult

➢ The Bible doesn't tell the whole story of what happened when Moses was escaping to the Red Sea with the Egyptians right behind him. When Moses asked for help, God said he had some good news and some bad news. The good news was that he would part the Red Sea and let Moses and his people escape. Moses asked him, "What's the bad news?" And God said, "First you have to file an environmental impact statement."

Greed Is Hard to Overcome

➢ An old woman was swindled out of her life savings by a promoter of a crooked investment scheme. She went to the Securities and Exchange Commission and told their consumer affairs representative about it. He knew about the scam and he scolded her. He asked her why she didn't check

with their office first, and she said, "I would have—
but I was afraid you would tell me not to give him
the money."

Caring in Health Care

➤ At our health maintenance organization, as at
many others, lots of elderly people who have nothing to do come in just to tell the doctor their troubles.
One woman came every day. There was nothing
wrong with her, but everyone listened patiently and
actually looked forward to her visits. One day she
didn't show up. When she came in the next day,
everyone asked, "Where were you yesterday? We
missed you." She said, "To tell you the truth, I
was sick."

Lack of Caring in Health Care

➤ A student nurse answered the phone at the hospital and a very irate caller demanded to know
the condition of a Mr. Green. The nurse was very
cooperative and found the patient's chart, and
reported that Mr. Green had been in poor condition, but had spent a restful night and was steadily
improving. When she heard a sigh of relief, she realized she had better find out who was calling, so
she asked. The man said, "This is Mr. Green. I've been
here two weeks and my doctor won't tell me anything!"

The Necessity of Having Health Insurance

➤ A friend of mine was always arguing with his wife
over money, so finally he decided to let her handle
it. Two months later she told him she'd saved
enough for them to go on a skiing vacation. They

went to a deluxe resort and had a beautiful room, but he was worried. He asked her, "Where did you get the money for this?" She just said, "I got rid of something we never used." They went out on the slopes and just when everything seemed perfect, he had an accident and broke his foot. At the hospital, his wife was very upset, and he said, "What's the matter? I'll be out of here in no time." She said, "I sure hope so. Remember when I told you I got rid of something we never used? It was our hospital insurance."

Honesty Is Sometimes a Matter of Technicalities

➤ The son of a successful businessman had just finished his MBA program at a prestigious school, and his father was giving him a little advice about the real world. He said, "Son, always remember that in business, as in life, honesty is the best policy. And I'd urge you to keep up on your corporation law, because you'll be amazed at what you can do and still be honest!"

Ignorance Is Bliss

➤ I was at my favorite Italian restaurant for lunch and was surprised to see a Vietnamese waiter come and take my order in perfect Italian. I called the owner over and said, "Where did you find a Vietnamese waiter that speaks Italian so well?" She said, "Ssshhh . . . he thinks we're teaching him English."

Inflation Is Always a Threat

➤ A man died and had his body frozen. When he came back 50 years later, the first thing he did was call his broker. He said, "How are my stocks doing?" The broker said, "Your IBM is now worth $6,000 a share, your AT & T is at $3,500, and your GM is at $4,050." The man said, "That's great, I'm a millionaire!" Just then the telephone operator broke in and said, "Your first three minutes are up—please deposit another $500."

Go to the Source for Information

➢ An executive received a call from another company's personnel office concerning a former employee. They asked, "How long did he work for you?" The executive said, "Oh, about three days." The caller said, "But he told us he was with you for two years." The executive said, "That's just it—he was."

The Value of Inside Information

➢ The CEO of a prominent takeover target was in the company cafeteria when an employee noticed he was really wolfing down a big lunch. The employee said to a co-worker, "Gee, he eats like there's no tomorrow." The other employee said, "Maybe he knows something."

Be Sure You Have Complete Information

➢ The wife of a busy executive complained to her friend that she never saw her husband because he was home late every night, and she was bored staying home alone. The friend said, "You just need to get out and exercise a little. It'll keep you busy and relax you, too. Why don't you get a bicycle and ride it ten miles every night this week—you'll feel a lot better." The next week the friend got another call from her. The friend said, "Well, did you take my advice?" The other woman said, "Yes I did . . . now I feel worse than ever." "Why?" "I'm 70 miles from home!"

Initiative Is Not Properly Encouraged

➤ The vice president called a junior executive into the VP's office and told him, "I notice you seem more interested in your work than anyone else. You work late every night, you pay attention to the slightest details, and you're always willing to take on new projects." The junior exec thought he was about to be promoted, but the VP said, "So . . . you're fired. It's people like you who go out and start their own business."

Innovation Is Necessary in Marketing

➤ A canning company that was trying to sell white salmon was having difficulty breaking into the market because of the established popularity of pink salmon. Finally they came up with the solution. On the label of every can it said, "This salmon guaranteed not to turn pink in the can."

Interpreting Data Is Tricky

➤ I heard of one firm who had hired a consultant to come in and determine why they were losing money. When he showed up he asked one employee, "What do you do around here?" The woman said, "Nothing." He then asked another employee, "What do you do?" He also said, "Nothing." The consultant said, "Just as I thought . . . too much duplication of work."

➢ A lion was taking a poll to see if he was still the king of the jungle. He went to a monkey and said, "Who's the king of the jungle?" The monkey said, "You are, of course." He went to a giraffe and asked him, "Who's the king of the jungle?" The giraffe said, "Why, you are." Then he went to an elephant. He again asked, "Who's the king of the jungle?" The elephant said nothing, but picked the lion up in its trunk and threw him against a tree. Then it stepped on him several times and kicked him into a clearing. The lion staggered away and said, "Geez, you didn't have to get so upset just because you didn't know the answer!"

First Examine Yourself Before Making Judgements

➢ Two Wall Street operators caught one of their clerks stealing $100 from petty cash. One of the partners wanted to fire the boy on the spot. The other, though, took a more understanding attitude. He told his partner, "After all, we started out on a small scale ourselves."

Know Thyself and Stay within Yourself

➢ A woman bought shoes in the most fashionable store in the city. A few days later she returned there saying she couldn't walk in the shoes. The manager said, "Madam—people who have to walk don't buy shoes in this store."

The Value of Specialized Knowledge

➢ A new computer that was practically running the business in one office had suddenly stopped working. No one could locate the trouble, let alone correct it, so they were forced to call in a consultant from the manufacturer. When he arrived he opened his briefcase, took out a small hammer, and tapped the side of the computer. It started working immediately, When he submitted his bill for $500, the office manager was outraged. He said, "All you did was tap it with a hammer. I want an itemized bill!" The consultant took back the bill and wrote on the bottom: "Tapping computer with hammer—$1. Knowing where to tap—$499."

Management Is Not Perfect

➤ I remember one manager who complained that he'd have to fire a particular employee. He said, "She keeps asking me what we're going to do about the simplest problems—and it gets embarrassing to keep saying I don't know."

➤ The president of a manufacturing firm walked into his warehouse and saw a young man lounging against a box, reading a newspaper. He asked the boy, "How much do you make a week?" The kid said, "Two hundred dollars, sir." The president took $200 out of his wallet and said, "Here's a week's pay. Now get out." Then he found the foreman and said, "When did you hire that kid?" The foreman said, "I didn't. He was waiting for a receipt for the packages he delivered."

Both Sides Can Benefit from Negotiating

➤ A man had been in the army for one week and he asked the captain for a three-day pass. The officer was outraged. He said, "You've only been here one week and you want a three-day pass? You'll have to earn it! You'll have to do something spectacular for it!" That afternoon the soldier came back to the base driving an enemy tank. The captain was amazed. He said, "How did you do it?" The soldier said, "Easy. I was in my tank, and I saw the enemy tank coming at me. I put out my white flag, and he put out his. We talked. I said, 'You want a three-day pass?' He said, 'Yeah!' So we exchanged tanks."

Negotiating Can Be Frustrating

➢ A man needing new glasses went to the finest eye specialist in the state. He said, "What can you do for me?" The doctor said, "For $1000 I'll do surgery on your eyes and you won't need glasses anymore." The man said, "How about something cheaper?" The doctor said, "For $200 I'll fit you with the latest in contact lenses—you'll never even know they're there." The man said, "Anything cheaper?" The doctor was getting annoyed, but said, "For $100 I'll give you regular glasses—with designer frames." The man said, "That's still too much." The doctor said, "If you didn't want to spend any money, you could have gone to another doctor. You knew I was expensive—why did you come to me, anyway?" The man said, "When it comes to my health, I never skimp."

Don't Overlook the Obvious

➢ A customs officer at the Mexican border noticed a man coming across one day on a bicycle with two small sacks tied to the handlebars. He naturally got suspicious and asked him to open the sacks, but when he did he found nothing but sand in them.

This went on every day for the next month. Each time he'd stop the bicycle and open the sacks, and he'd find only sand. Much later, he ran into the biker in a bar in Tijuana. He talked to him. "Come on, I know you were smuggling something all that time. I won't tell, I'm just curious now— what was it?" The other man said, "Bicycles."

Dangers of Overcapitalization

➤ A business owner went to a psychiatrist and said, "Doctor, I've got serious problems. I own a $40,000 car, I live in a $300,000 house, and I'm thinking of opening a new factory." The doctor said, "Then what's your problem?" The patient said, "Well, I never gross more than $100 a week."

One Person's Problem Is Another's Opportunity

➤ Many years ago, a large American shoe manufacturer sent two of its sales reps out to the wilds of the Australian outback to see if they could drum up some new business among the aborigines. Both sales reps noticed that none of the natives wore shoes. The first one immediately wired home and said, "Returning on next plane, no business here. Natives don't wear shoes." The other rep also sent a wire: "Quick, send millions of shoes, all sizes. Natives not wearing any."

Partnerships Are Not Always Equal

➤ A chicken and a pig wanted to go into business together but couldn't decide what to do. The chicken said, "Let's open a ham and eggs restaurant—it's a natural for us!" The pig said, "Oh sure. . .it's a day's work for you, but for me it's a real sacrifice!"

Don't Be Penny Wise and Pound Foolish

➤ A manager was complaining to the vice president. "My salespeople are always asking for expense money. Like Smith—last week he wanted $100. Yesterday he wanted $200. Today he wanted $250." The vice president said, "That's crazy. What does he do with it all?" The manager said, "I don't know— I never give him any."

The Value of Persistence

➤ A salesman visited the office of a very difficult potential buyer at the end of a busy day. He was let in just before five o'clock and the prospect said, "You ought to feel honored. Do you know that so far today I've refused to see twelve salesmen?" The other man said, "I know—I'm them."

The Importance of One's Perspective

➤ An Israeli visiting China wanted very much to find a synagogue and worship on the Sabbath. He searched all over the city he was in before finally finding one in an old part of town. During the service, he noticed that the Chinese rabbi kept staring at him the entire time. Afterward, the rabbi approached him. He asked, "Are you of our faith?" The man said, "Why yes, rabbi." The other said, "That's funny—you don't look Jewish."

➤ The owner of a New York clothing store went on a vacation to Europe, and when he came back he described the entire trip to his tailor in great detail.

He told him, "I even went to the Vatican and saw the Pope." The tailor was impressed. He said, "The Pope! What does he look like?" The other man said, "Oh, I figure a size 38 short."

➤ We shouldn't be like the priest who got tired while on a walk in a strange neighborhood. He went into a church and fell asleep. A sexton roused him and said they were closing up. The priest said, "But the cathedral never closes." The sexton said, "This isn't the cathedral, it's a Presbyterian church." The priest looked around and said, "Isn't that St. Matthew over there?" The sexton said, "It is." "And isn't that St. Mark, and St. Thomas?" The sexton said, "Yes." The priest said, "Tell me . . . when did they all become Presbyterian?"

Poor Planning

➤ One of our technicians told me she was working on a solution that would dissolve anything. When I asked her what she was going to store it in, she said, "We'll work on that later."

The Value of Planning

➤ I remember a court case where a witness was called to testify on an automobile accident. The lawyer said, "Did you actually see the accident?" The witness said, "Yes." The lawyer said, "And how far away were you when the accident happened?" The witness said, "Twenty-one feet, nine and one quarter inches." The lawyer just looked at the witness for a minute and then said, "Will you please tell the court how you knew it was exactly twenty-one feet, nine and one quarter inches?" The other said, "When it happened, I took out a tape measure and checked the distance . . . because I knew some damn lawyer was going to ask me that question!"

Positive Attitude

➤ A friend of mine who had just celebrated a wedding anniversary was complaining to another fellow. He said, "When I first got married, I'd come home and my wife would bring me the paper and the dog would run around barking at me. After ten years now, things have changed a bit. The dog brings me the paper and my wife barks at me." His friend said, "What are you complaining about? You're getting the same service."

Identifying the Real Problems

➤ One entrepreneur had a terrible time getting start-up money. He was turned down time after time by every bank he went to. Finally he found a private investor—a wealthy old man willing to take a risk on a new business. The man gave him $50,000—and within three months he'd lost it and the business went nowhere. So he approached the man again and got another $50,000. Two months later, that was gone, and still there were no profits. He asked again and received another $50,000—and lost that too. Finally, he talked to one of his friends about his experience with his backer. The friend said, "There's only one thing to do. Get rid of him— he's bad luck for you!"

Promises Are Not Always Kept

➤ A new congressman was trying to appease a group of farmers because he was behind schedule in some of his campaign promises. He told them, "If you put a bull in a field with the cows one night, you wouldn't expect to see a lot of newborn calves the very next morning, would you?" One farmer called out, "No, but you'd expect to see a lot of contented faces!"

The Responsibility Is Not Mine

➤ I feel like the minister who was sitting next to a nervous little old lady on an airplane. The plane got caught in a storm and tossed around violently. The lady panicked and said to the minister, "You're a man of God, can't you do something about this?" The minister said, "Lady, I'm in sales, not management."

Standards of Quality

➤ I was on the road and having trouble with my car, so I pulled into a service station just off the highway. I was a little leery about going to a place I didn't know, so I watched one of the mechanics work for a while. He was amazing. He changed the oil without spilling a drop. He wiped his hands before touching the upholstery, and he pulled the car out of the garage very slowly and carefully. I was so impressed that I said to the guy pumping gas, "Boy, your mechanic really does a good job, doesn't he?" He said, "Why not? It's his car."

The World's Greatest Salesman

➤ A man went into a clothing store and said to the owner, "I need a job really bad—can you hire me as a saleman?" The owner said, "I'll tell you what. I'm going out to lunch. If you can sell that ugly plaid suit over there by the time I get back, you're hired.'" The suit was the worst-looking thing he'd

ever seen, but he was desperate, so he agreed to
try. An hour later the manager came back and he
found the store in shambles: racks turned over,
clothing scattered everywhere—but the suit was
sold. He said to the saleman, "What happened? Did
you have some kind of trouble in here?" He said,
"Oh, I had no trouble with the customer who bought
that suit. But what a tough seeing eye dog!"

Sexism in Hiring

➤ An executive hiring a secretary called in a psychologist to help him decide. The psychologist tested
50 applicants, and eliminated all but three. He
met with each of them to administer the final test
while the executive watched. He asked the first one,
"How much is three and three?" She said, "Six."
He asked the second the same question and she
said, "It could be 33." The third one answered, "It
could be six and it could be 33." When they had
left the room, the psychologist said to the executive,
"Well, the first woman gave the logical answer. The
second one showed imagination. The third one
showed both practicality and imagination. Which
one are you going to hire?" He said, "That's easy.
I'll take the blonde in the short skirt."

Sexism on the Job

➤ When a female executive asked her boss for a raise,
he said, "But you're already making as much as
any of the male executives—and they've all got
families with two and three kids." She said, "Look,
I thought we were being paid for what we did here
on the job—not what we do on our own time."

Statistics Can't Always Be Trusted

➤ On my first day in the city, I took a cab downtown.
I asked the driver what his average tip was, and
he said, "Five dollars." So I gave him five dollars
and I said, "Gee, you must do all right driving a
cab in this town." He said, "Not really. This is the
first average tip I've gotten this week."

Stockbrokers

➤ A stockbroker was complaining to a colleague
about his daughter's recent marriage. He said, "I
spent $40,000 on her education and she married a
guy who makes only $20,000 a year." The other
broker said, "What are you complaining about?
You're still getting a 50-percent return on your
money."

Tactfulness Can Help in a Delicate Situation

➤ A friend of mine got a call at the office from his
pregnant wife. She said, "I've finally decided on a
name for the new baby. Let's call her Abigail." Her
husband thought it was a terrible name, but he
said, "That's nice. I used to know a girl named
Abigail, and that name always calls back fond mem-
ories." The wife was quiet for a moment, and then
she said, "You know, dear, maybe Mary is nicer."

➤ The author John Steinbeck best described tact-
fulness in a story about two men discussing the
town of Green Bay, Wisconsin. The first man said,
"It's a real nice place." The other man said, "What's
nice about it? The only things ever to come out
of Green Bay are football players and ugly girls."

The first man got angry. He said, "Wait a minute—
my wife is from Green Bay!" The other man said,
"Oh? What position does she play?"

Tax Deductions Can Be Creative

➤ The owner of a small pizza place was called in for
an IRS audit. As the agent was going over the books,
she found there were several trips to Europe that
had been deducted as business expenses. She said,
"Why does a pizza maker have to take business
trips to Europe?" The man said, "I forgot to tell
you—we deliver."

Keeping Up with Technology

➤ Two executives from a high-tech firm spent most of
their spare time trying to outdo each other with
the latest and best of everything. So when one
bought a car phone, the other naturally got one for
himself and promptly called his friend. He said,
"Hi. I'm calling your car from my car." His friend
said, "Could you hold on—I'm on the other line."

Time Is Relative

➤ A young man in China recently applied for a visa
to come to America. He was told, "It is impossible
at present. Come back in a year." The man said,
"Morning or afternoon?"

Timing Is Critical

➤ A 75-year-old man was reading in his hotel room
when he heard a knock on the door. He opened
it and a beautiful young woman said, "Sorry, I

must have the wrong room." He said, "You've got
the right room, but you're 40 years too late."

➤ I was visiting Windsor, outside of London, and a bus
took a group of us to a rather famous spot. One passenger asked the guide, "What happened here?" The
guide said, "This is where the Magna Carta was
signed." The tourist said, "When?" The guide said,
"1215." The tourist looked at his watch and said
to his wife, "Darn, we missed it by twenty minutes."

Unions: Asking Too Much

➤ The union president had bargained an unbeliev-
able contract only six months earlier, and now he
was demanding to renegotiate. The company president said, "In your last deal you got basic pay
doubled, four coffee breaks, hospitalization for second cousins, birthdays off . . . now what do you
want?" The union man said, "I want a guarantee you won't go broke."

Unions: Solidarity

➤ A union president died and approached the gates
of heaven. The gatekeeper asked him, "Do you
wish to enter?" The union man looked at a band of
angels passing by the gate and said, "Well, after seeing them I'm not sure." The gatekeeper asked him why
and he said, "In my whole lifetime, I never crossed
a picket line, and I'll be damned if I'll start now."

Women Executives Must Be Recognized

➤ A pregnant executive was having trouble sleeping
at night so she asked her doctor for something to

help. He wanted to prescribe sleeping pills, but she said they didn't work on her. She asked for an especially strong sedative she had heard about for pregnant women. The doctor said, "But that's just for labor." She said, "Well, doctor, don't you have anything for management?"

The Disappearance of the Work Ethic

➢ I remember my grandfather telling me about looking for work when he was a young man. He said he once refused a job working in a factory ten hours a day, six days a week . . . because he didn't want a part-time job.

Workers Today Expect Interaction

➢ The boss approached his office manager and told him, "There's $1,000 missing from the safe, and you and I are the only ones who have the keys to it. So what have you got to say?" The office manager said, "Well, why don't we each put up $500 and forget about it?"

Index